Paranormal Investigation - The Basic's
By: Mark Davis

Visit our website at www.markoftheparanormal.com

Published August 2010 by MPDavis publishing
Media PA

Front cover art design by: Mark Davis

Printed in the United States of America

The dedication of this book is for my beautiful wife Jean, and our three amazing children Emily, Alli and Kyle; all of whom have been extremely supportive while I have traveled through the many different aspects of the paranormal. I love you all so very, very much.

I sincerely wish to thank Anthony and Barbara Selletti whose help and support of this effort has been never ending. Their input was invaluable to this publication.

Chapter	Page

Introduction

The purpose of this book is to introduce you to the basics of paranormal investigation. There are many means and methods currently being employed by a wide variety of investigators out there; some perhaps better than others. One thing for sure is that we are all learning and advancing this field of research on a daily basis.

This is not the only way to investigate or report, but it is a way that I have used for years that seems to work well. I have developed some methods of doing things based on the training and interaction that I have had with other investigators. Some I have taken more from than others but they all had an influence on me in some way. I have also seen investigators go out there after they have just watched a few television programs and decided they know what they are doing. Hopefully you will not be a part of the latter. From the mere fact that you have picked up this book is a testament to you trying to find a proper way to investigate, or simply stated a way that will work best for you.

Okay, I know what you're thinking, who is this guy and what makes him different (or more knowledgeable) than any of the other researchers out there? I have been researching the paranormal since the late 1990's. With the advent of the internet I was able to delve deeper into this field which eventually led me to join a group of investigators. The first group I joined had a major impact on how I approach the paranormal.

After a couple of years with them I decided to step out and start my own group. This was truly an eye opener. I had no idea what to expect or how to actually begin. This led to a new research "how to" project. Well, the group I started is still going strong today and I recently left it to concentrate on finishing this project. I'm also pursuing some new endeavors within the paranormal field.

When I started my former group, I had to establish a means and methods of operation and investigation which at the time I didn't realize laid the foundation for this book. After years of training people and showing them the methods described here, many of them suggested that I put them into a book from which others could learn from. You hold in your hands the fruit of that labor.

Whether you are just starting out or if you're an experienced investigator, there may be some things inside that you may not have been aware. I hope you all can learn something from this book as I continue to learning more from others as well.

1. So You Want to be a Paranormal Investigator?

Let's start by saying that after reading this book, you will be on your way to becoming a paranormal investigator. Obviously, practical experience will make you a better investigator, and that will come in time.

There are many means to an end; you just need to find what works the best for you. Is everything I cover here the only way or the absolute answer on everything? Unequivocally NO! As in everything in life, there are many different approaches to investigation techniques and reporting methods. With the key points I will share with you here, you can begin to build a solid foundation and get comfortably moving in a positive direction.

Now, before you jump up and run out there with a voice recorder and camera in hand, you need to ask yourself a few important questions:

- Why do **"I"** want to be a paranormal investigator?
- What do **"I"** want to learn from doing this?
- Am **"I"** doing this just to see a ghost or do **"I"** want to learn what's really happening?
- Do **"I"** want to help people that need help with the paranormal?

If you notice all of the **"I"**s are bold type. Before you can get started as a researcher, you need to understand yourself and what you want to get out of this field. If you cannot address these issues honestly, then you are not going to be able to offer assistance to anyone who may need it. We all want to learn more about the nature of anomalies, but we will also be given the opportunity to help people as we do our research. Hopefully that will become your driving force.

I will try to cover all aspects of an investigation for you within these pages. Will this cover everything you may encounter? No, it will not. Each case is different and you never truly know what you will encounter until you are in a situation. This will, however, show you how to get started.

Getting Started:

Here are two important questions. What you want to get out of doing research in the paranormal field? That's a pretty straight forward question which can have many different answers, depending on the individual. The second question is a bit more philosophical. How well do you understand yourself? So with those thoughts, we'll get started working on the second question.

Understanding yourself seems pretty easy to do, right? Be honest with yourself and know what you can and cannot do. No two people are alike and others may be able to do more than you can. Your communication skills are going to be a key factor in your development. When you become involved in a team situation, you need to share your strengths as well as weaknesses and become familiar with theirs; both physical and mental.

If you have a bad leg and have issues when you are walking around for an extended period of time, your team needs to know this so they can "cover" for you if needed. There may be another position on that particular investigation that you can fill with less discomfort. All positions on a team are valuable, so don't take this as a judgment of your contribution. Remember, we should be challenged in our work, not be abused by it.

When you are successful in communicating your limitations, then you will have opened the door to more enjoyment while doing this kind of work. I have told all of the "newbie's" over the years that if they didn't ask, we couldn't answer. So feel free to ask any questions that you may have. The only wrong question is the one left unasked.

The other side to this is when you receive an answer and you do not understand it, say so. Ask for a more definitive answer. Keep asking until you understand. This is where the analogy, "we are only as strong as our weakest link" comes into play. Never pretend to understand something when you don't, that will only cause a problem later on.

If you do not understand certain points that you have read or have been taught, let it be known. You never want to enter a site not understanding something that the others believe you do. You will only hurt yourself and your team if you do that. When you effectively communicate to your team that you do not understand, they will more than likely place you with an individual that is stronger in that area so you will be able to learn and hopefully understand it more clearly. I can't stress this enough.

A few thoughts as we begin:

Hollywood has created an image of a haunted house that many people believe to be accurate. When starting out please note that this is not the case. Hollywood is trying to entertain you. Typically, spirits do not want to do that. Can you run into some intense things when doing this? Without a doubt you can. This is why you need to understand what you may experience and be better able to handle the situation.

Most investigators that have been doing this for awhile don't normally get frightened when something occurs. Everyone can and will get startled from time to time. As in all professions, we need to act accordingly and have control of our feelings and emotions. If you were a client and a paranormal investigator ran out of your home screaming into the night, how would you feel? Probably not too good, so always try to keep control of yourself when investigating. There is nothing wrong with asking your partner to get you out of a location if you do not feel comfortable.

What will you come across once you have decided to stay, try to learn and help people? Well let's start by saying like attracts like. If you go out and you're in a bad frame of mind, you will attract someone or something that has the same mind frame. So always go out with a positive attitude, if you don't have a good attitude, then don't go out. I don't think that point can be made any simpler.

How do I know that what I am going into is safe?

There are two points that need to be mentioned for this. First, you never know what you may encounter. It is always a good idea to err on the side of caution. Second the group leadership should have knowledge of what is happening and have made a determination on the level of activity as to the severity of the haunting.

Before you begin, there needs to be some delineation discussed within your group as to whether you will be involved with demonic hauntings or not.

Make no mistake, the demonic is real and exists. If you choose to become a member of a group that will only handle demonic cases, remember that this is a life decision; once you begin there is no turning around. That being said, if your group's leadership does not handle that type of haunting then you should feel comfortable that they would never put you in that sort of situation.

Why do we say this? Because as we all have been taught that there is good and bad out there and they weren't kidding. As a new paranormal investigator, never try to take on a "bad" entity. It's like Bill Murray's character in "Caddy Shack" challenging Tiger Woods to an 18 hole play-off. You will be setting yourself up for failure. You need to contact someone that has more experience and knowledge in dealing with this type of entity. You would not be doing anyone any favors by trying to resolve that kind of situation alone.

On site:

One thing you should not be given any information on a case, typically only the team leader for that case would know what is happening. The reason for this is to eliminate any predispositions to certain conclusions.

One of the worst questions I have heard from many investigators is "Give me a sign of your presence". As the old saying goes, be careful for what you ask for or you may get more than what you can handle! This type of question is open ended and that sign could be something that you never expected or wanted.

So it is better to be more specific, for example ask for the light knock, that you do, to be replicated. There is more control with doing that and it will be safer for you. Also remember that the client will need to live with what you do, if you create a situation that will anger whatever is there, you can always leave, but they may not have that option. So be respectful. Whatever you ask to happen can occur after you have left. If it does you can scare your client even more.

Generally there are three types of hauntings that you are likely to encounter on an investigation; intelligent, residual and ones that are referred to as demonic.

An intelligent haunting is one where the spirit may interact with you. They are aware of their surroundings and are usually not confined to one spot. They are looking for people to notice them, and often they end up scaring people who do not understand what they are trying to communicate.

The residual haunting is one where the event has been recorded into the surrounding area. It is an impression or energy "snapshot" made in time. When the situation is right, this event will play back similar to a DVD. No matter how hard you try, this "recorded" event will not interact with you.

The last would be nothing but trouble for you. As I have said, if you come into contact with a nonhuman entity, or a demonic spirit get immediate help from someone who has the knowledge to handle it.

So now you are in the house with so much happening to others in the team. What should you do? Well you should continue with what you are doing until asked for help to document something in another location. Also when the fray is happening with you, be calm and pay attention to what is going on. Use your equipment and investigate. If you need help ask for it. If you need to leave, do so calmly with your partner.

Organizational skills are important:

Organization is very important when you are on an investigation. Hopefully you will be with an established team that has protocols in place, so that everyone understands what is expected from its members during an investigation. If you are going to do this on your own, we have a chapter here to help you out with some ideas on how to organize your investigation.

As you begin your training, you may be reading and searching the Internet for a wide variety of information. If you just print things out and leave them in a folder, you will find it difficult to use these items as points of reference when you need them.

I suggest the use of a three ring binder with divider tabs that can be labeled, this helps with the organization of topics. I personally have quite a few of them which I reference often. A fellow investigator does this and keeps a list of titles on their computer, so they can keep track of them when she searches the net.

What do they do with all of that equipment?

What should you bring with you on an investigation? You probably have seen all of this great equipment being used on television and listed all over paranormal investigators' websites. You might be thinking that you'll need to take out loans to get started. It is true that the high-end equipment is neat, but it can be really expensive.

My advice? Start out small. All you really need is a book to take notes, an open mind and a camera. If you decide to continue, other equipment will eventually follow. Just remember the basics when using a camera, in chapter 5 we discuss the use of a camera.

We have a complete section on the basic equipment within this book for you, where we will discuss how certain pieces work and the important things to know about each one of them. For someone that is just starting out I suggest the same pieces of equipment, a good digital camera (greater than 5 mega pixels) and a digital recorder with a time stamp feature. These pieces will be very beneficial to you throughout your investigative career.

If you are with an established organization they should have a variety of equipment for you to use and learn. As time goes on you will begin to find some that you like and others that you don't. When this starts and you have made the commitment to continue, you may want to then consider purchasing some of your own favorite items. I strongly suggest that you wait until you have had the opportunity to use equipment before you go out and just buy some.

What does it take to become a Paranormal Investigator?

To be a paranormal investigator you must have an open mind and be able to look at all possibilities before jumping to the conclusion that a location is haunted. You should have a very detailed method on how you conduct and review your investigations evidence and what control methods you have in place to insure that fraud is not taking place either on your team or at the location.

However the most important tool for anybody wanting to do this properly, you already have and that is yourself. What you believe and who you are all play a major factor in this field. You need to learn and understand what your body is telling you. Once you do that, you will begin the foundation on what you build upon. Starting with a solid foundation you can't go wrong.

Your body is a pretty amazing tool and has many different defense mechanisms built in at no extra charge. So be sure to pay attention to what your body is telling you. Impressions are very important. If the hair on the back of your neck is going up, and it's not normal, this could be something paranormal happening. Be sure to take notes, photos etc.

If you are sitting on a chair in the corner of a client's living room and you are feeling extremely sad or angry or just have an uncomfortable feeling. It's important to note it. It may have no meaning to you at the time, but that could have been the chair of the late Aunt Emma and you were picking up her feelings! Don't be surprised, that will happen at some point, you just need to recognize it.

When you go out for the first time there is no doubt that you will be excited to go and see something. You can be headed into the house on the corner that has many stories associated with it, so you are now pumped up to be going. While you are there, nothing happens.

Now you are feeling let down. Why am I telling you this? Simple; never expect anything to happen. When you do you will be let down and you will also think there is no merit to any of this. When you enter without any expectations you cannot be let down and you are more open to what is going on.

I would also like to touch on a couple of related areas. I have been on cases where absolutely nothing is happening and one or two investigators have decided to "investigate" a bedroom or an area with a sofa and have actually fallen asleep. Obviously this is not acceptable, if you are that tired you should not have come out to investigate in the first place.

The last thing I would like to discuss is boredom; yes boredom. Remember we are in a location for a short amount of time and the client is there all of the time. Activity does not occur because you are there. More than likely you will not come up with much evidence on your first investigation to the site. When that is happening I have seen many people start to provoke. I am not a proponent of this approach, especially when being done in a confrontational or open ended manner.

Knowledge is Power:

No one can hope to know everything, no matter how long you study something. Do yourself a favor and read everything you can. The internet is loaded with a wealth of information that can enlighten you on all aspects of ghost hunting. Just remember to be discriminating. Not everything on the internet is good or practical.

Find a mentor. Ask a ghost group in your area for advice on what to read or how they conduct a paranormal investigation. Ask if they would they show you or let you sit in on a meeting or an investigation.

Be aware that most established groups would not likely allow the latter due to possible evidence contamination. If you can join their group, let them know that you are interested in learning how to properly do an investigation.

When you are with the group, watch them while they are conducting the investigation. Look to see how the team members interact with each other and with the client. Take note if the group is organized or not; if it's is all over the place, you may end up learning bad habits. A group that respects each other and the location they're in, says a lot about their characters and commitment to the science.

No one truly knows what a ghost is, and until we find that irrefutable piece of evidence that no one can argue against we may never know. What we do as investigators is look for that piece of evidence while we help people along the way. Many people think they are experts in this field but we are all always learning and developing as we move forward.

Now you know that you want to help people and to learn. You also know what you may possibly come across and you still decide to go out there and try this.

My suggestion would be to become a member of an established organization. They will teach all you need to know on how to conduct a proper investigation. What if you don't have any such organizations near you and you want to try this anyway. Then be as smart as you can. Do not go anywhere without permission, alone or without a way to communicate with other team members. Carry your cell phone, what if someone is hurt, you'll need that.

If this is something you decide to do, remember to be careful and respectful. Treat people as you would want to be treated. Remember that you will be representing more than just yourself out there; you will be representing the larger community of paranormal investigators.

2. A Brief History of Ghost Hunting

To understand where we are going in this field we need some understanding of where we, as a research field, came from. Throughout human history men and women have believed in an afterlife. Ghosts were often believed to be departed relatives, deceased people looking for vengeance or trapped souls paying for bad deeds committed in life.

In the early days of science, a conscious decision was made to leave the realm of spirituality with the church. With this decision came the lack of an understanding in the spiritual world. If this had been addressed by science back in the time of say, Galileo; then the field of paranormal research would have developed with all other scientific studies, rather than being judged as a pseudo science.

Being that the church had taken over the realm of the spirit, and that you could be accused of being a witch that came with a death sentence, nobody wanted to admit they saw a spirit. But as time went on they became more aware of spirits and how to talk about them (and not get burned at the stake).

This was a time in history where many people started to have "visions". This was an accepted way to tell the tale of a ghost visitation without being accused of witchcraft. In our modern society, with ghosts seemingly turning up everywhere, it has become more acceptable to discuss such topics in polite company. Indeed, try and find someplace that you don't hear someone sharing stories of some anomalous experience, especially since the advent of the World Wide Web (WWW). I'll add a caveat here; I know a couple of investigators who have experienced a lot of flak for their involvement in paranormal investigations. Common sense should be used when you openly discuss this field.

Most of the earliest reports of hauntings were limited to eye witness accounts but as science and technology grew, so did the quest to find proof of life after death.

Most of the time, supernatural happenings were found to have natural explanations, sometimes they didn't. Skeptics wanted to disprove ghosts and believers wanted to prove they did exist. Everyone loves a mystery and ghosts present one of the biggest mysteries to humankind since the beginning of time.

One of the very first ghost hunting investigations can be traced back to the 1st century A. D. A man named Athenodoros rented a house in Athens, Greece; to explore rumors of a haunting within the house. The fist night he stayed at the house, he reported seeing an old man with bound feet and hands. The old man rattled chains and coaxed Athenodoros to follow him. Athenodoros complied and followed the old man until he vanished. Athenodoros marked the spot where the vision disappeared and had officials dig there. Eventually, shackled bones were found, buried and the old man never appeared again.

The tales of ghosts and hauntings continue throughout history and amid the myriad of cultures. In the 1600s the chaplain of Charles II, Joseph Glanvill investigated ghostly activity in the British Isles.

Glanvill's most famous case was the Phantom Drummer of Tedworth. The drummer haunted an English family. Making drumming sounds, beating night after night. It would also violently hit furniture and smashed a bedstead to pieces. Only when a clergyman came to visit did it stop.

In the 1800s the Chase family tomb of Barbados caught the attention of the press. Coffins seemed to be moved, rearranged and even thrown against walls. The entrance to the tomb was sealed with mortar and the governor's mark until the next death in the Chase family.

Before the tomb was opened for the burial, a thorough inspection of the vault from the outside was made. It was found to be as strong as ever. The mortar seal was examined and was intact and the marks in the mortar were untouched.

As the door of the tomb was being pulled away, a strange sound came from within the crypt. To everyone's amazement, the coffin containing the body of Dorcas Chase, dead for eight years, was leaning against the marble door.

Another coffin of Mary Anna Maria Chase, inside the tomb for 12 years, had been flung so violently against the left side wall that it had chipped away a piece of it. The rest of the coffins had also been disturbed and the sand covering the floor showed no trace of... anything. The Chase family then emptied the vault and today it remains empty and as far as we know, quiet.

Perhaps the biggest phase in paranormal investigation came onto the scene in the mid 1800s, as a growing fascination in the occult spiritualist movement grew during the Victorian era. Some of the better known and influential were:

The Fox Sisters: Kate and Margaretta

Generally considered to have initiated the Modern Spiritualist Movement, the three Fox sisters (Kate, Margaretta, and Leah) of Hydesville, New York are credited with starting the trend of mediumship or communication with the dead.

On December 11, 1847, John Fox, along with his wife Margaret and their daughters, moved into a house that had a reputation of being "haunted". In fact, the prior tenant, Michael Weakman, moved out of the house because of the inexplicable tapping and other noises.

It became quickly apparent to the Fox family, that they were not alone in occupying the place after they began to be disturbed by strange sounds and activities at night. The children were so alarmed that they refused to sleep apart and were taken into the bedroom of their parents. No one could figure out the source of the "activity".

Finally, on March 31st, young Kate Fox made history by challenging the mysterious unseen power to repeat the snaps of her fingers. The sound instantly followed her with the same number of raps. As time went on, the girls would ask questions of departed souls and answers would come in the form of knocks and table taps.

Upon further inquiry, it was ascertained that the spirit's name was Charles B. Rosna and that he had been a peddler who stayed at the house five years prior to these incidents.

The sisters moved to the houses of other family members, but the disturbances continued. It was suggested by a friend to try conversing with the spirits using the alphabet (a form of Quija board divination) and they received remarkable communications.

Many people believed the sisters were authentic, however, many did not. Some believed that the Fox sisters were taking advantage of the bereaved.

Helena P. Blatavsky (1831-1891)

Helena Blatavsky was a renowned medium during the 1870s and one of the founders the Theosophical Society, which encouraged the study of comparative religion, philosophy, science and the investigation of the unexplained laws of nature and the (psychical) powers latent in man.

Helena grew up amid a culture rich in spirituality and traditional Russian mythologies, which introduced her to the realm of the supernatural.

She was a world traveler between1848 to 1858 and it was during her stay in Cairo in the early 1870s that Blavatsky established herself as a medium (based upon the belief that spirits of the dead residing in the spirit realm could be contacted by people through an intermediate) and began holding séances.

In 1873, she immigrated to New York City and impressed people with her professed psychic abilities.

Henry Sidgwick (1838-1900)

Henry Sidgwick was one of the six founders and first president of the Society of Psychical Research or SPR whose purpose was to understand "events and abilities commonly described as psychic or paranormal by promoting and supporting important research in this area" and to "examine allegedly paranormal phenomena in a scientific and unbiased way."

Edmund Gurney (1847-1888)

Edmund was an English psychologist and psychical researcher and member of the SPR. He wanted to investigate the persistence of the conscious human personality after the death of the body. With Frank Podmore, Frederic William Henry Myers (a member of the Theosophical Society), created the landmark volumes entitled, Phantasms of the Living, a collection of first person accounts of possible cases telepathy. They argued that similar experiences occurred spontaneously in many recorded instances of deathbed visions.

Harry Price (1881-1948)

Harry Price is considered by most to be the father of the modern day paranormal investigator. There are several books documenting the achievements of Mr. Price along with his legacy. He was instrumental in bringing paranormal research to the attention of the general public. He truly was the first "Para-celebrity"

When Harry was 15, he and a friend locked themselves in a house thought to be haunted overnight. During the night they kept hearing footsteps upstairs. They set-up a camera at the base of the stairs and when they heard footsteps coming down the stairs they took a picture. When the plate was developed, it showed nothing but an empty staircase.

Price would always consider this as his first encounter with a ghost. He managed to give ghost research a place in the public eye and opened it up to those who don't fit into the categories of professional scientists, hard-headed skeptics, nor fall into the realm of gullible "true believer".

In 1908 Harry met and married a wealthy heiress named Constance Mary Knight. This allowed Harry to do something most everyone in this field dream of today, he became an independently wealthy paranormal investigator.

In England there existed the Society of Psychical Research or SPR. Within this society Price had many enemies due to his personality and his constant self promotion.

By the time that Price joined the SPR in 1920, he had already begun his career as Britain's most famous ghost investigator. He had spent many hours at alleged haunted houses and in the investigation of Spiritualist mediums. He was also an expert magician and soon made a name for himself within the SPR for using his magic skills to debunk fraudulent psychics, then in keeping with what was the main thrust of the current SPR investigations.

One of Price's first efforts exposed the work of spirit photographer William Hope, who was making a fortune taking portraits of people and these portraits always seemed to include the sitter's dead relatives. Price was sent to investigate and soon published his findings. He claimed that Hope used pre-exposed plates in his camera, which he learned by secretly switching the plates the photographer was using with plates of his own.

On afternoon while waiting for a train, Price met Stella Crenshaw. They struck up a conversation where she began telling Price the tales concerning the anomalous phenomenon that she had been experiencing for years. This consisted of moving objects, cold spots and knocking sounds. Price immediately asked if she would consider being a test subject for his psychical research.

Price was also an amateur inventor and had developed a device called the telekinetoscope. This device was basically a telegraph in a glass dome that would turn a light on when the key was depressed. He felt that anyone that was a psychic would be able to turn this light on without any difficulty.

From March through October 1923, Price and Stella conducted 13 separate séances in which they were sure to conducted in front of other witnesses, Stella managed to produce all sorts of strange, physical phenomena. During one séance, for example, she managed to levitate a table so high that the sitters had to rise out of their chairs to keep their hands upon it. Suddenly, three of the table legs broke away and the table itself folded and collapsed. Needless to say, this ended the sitting.

Harry is most famous for the investigation that he conducted at the Borley rectory. This series of investigations lead to two books entitled, "*The most haunted house in England*" (1940) and "*The end of the Borley rectory*" (1946). It was these books which placed Harry Price on the paranormal map.

Final words on the history of ghost hunting:

The media has also played a huge role in the popularity of paranormal investigations. Starting with the brief run of the television show, The Sixth Sense, during 1972-73, which centered on a professor who explored cases with a parapsychological basis with his psi talents, the movie, *The Entity* (based partially on a true story, a woman is tormented and sexually molested by an invisible demon in 1981), the successful release of the movie "Ghostbusters" in 1984 and the TV series, "Ghost Hunters" in 2004 paranormal research groups have reached a fevered pitch. Groups seem to be popping up everywhere and hopefully they are being trained into the proper way to conduct themselves.

In1922, Scientific American made an offer of $2500 for the first authentic spirit photograph made under test conditions, and/ or the first psychic to produce a "visible psychic manifestation." Harry Houdini was a member of the investigating committee. The first medium to be tested was George Valiantine, who claimed that in his presence spirits would speak through a trumpet that floated around a darkened room. For the test, Valiantine was placed in a room, the lights were extinguished, but unbeknownst to him his chair had been rigged to light a signal in an adjoining room if he ever left his seat. Because the light signals were tripped during his performance, Valiantine did not collect the award.

In more modern times, James Randi, a magician is best known as the world's most tireless investigator and demystifier of paranormal and pseudoscientific claims. Randi's long-standing challenge to psychics now stands as a $1,000,000 prize administered by the Foundation. It remains unclaimed.

Many individuals and groups have offered similar monetary awards for proof of the paranormal in an observed setting. These prizes have a combined value of over $2.4 million dollars, all still uncollected.

3. The History of EVP

Since the discovery of what has now come to be known as the Electronic Voice Phenomena (EVP), we have to give thanks for the efforts of many gifted researchers who, over the years have given their time and commitment in the face of much hostility.

Where did it all begin? More than likely with the discoveries made in the field of electronic communications by such inventors as Thomas Edison, Nikola Tesla, Oliver Lodge and Gueglielmo Marconi. These men of vision all held belief in an afterlife and the possibility of making contact with that world through electronic means.

Edison had his first lab at the age of ten and by the time of his death he had patented 1093 of his inventions. He also believed in a life after death, as can be determined by the many statements he made during his lifetime. "I will be going to a world beyond, whereby I shall continue the research where I left off".

It is also interesting to note that there was a blueprint found after his death for a machine which he believed could be used for making contact with that very place. No machine was ever found, so we have no means of knowing if he had actually built this.

Before the turn of the last Century: Austrian psychic researcher Baron Hellenbach predicted in his book *"Birth and Death the evolution of electromechanical means of communication"*. He foresaw that the content of the earliest contacts might suffer from the inherent difficulties of bridging a gulf between two dimensions and warned against undue optimism.

At the beginning of the Last Century: It is little known that Thomas Edison, Gueglielmo Marconi, and Nikola Tesla, the inventors and geniuses that had helped to harness electricity and lay the foundations upon which electronic communication has been based, spent the last years of their lives trying to develop devices for communicating with spirits.

1920`s: Hereward Carrington, a respected American psychical researcher notes in his book *"Psychic Oddities"* an occasion at which he was present when a 'disembodied' voice asked "Can you hear me?"

came out of a microphone in a sealed room at the radio recording studio when the rest of the building was empty. This was in the presence of an un-named medium and was heard by everyone else in the room. No-one could give any explanation.

The English writer Thorpe who had developed what he called 'Etheric Vision' (and wrote a book of the same name) whilst a prisoner in Germany, promised his readers details of mechanical means of detecting what he called 'The Voice Phenomenon' in a further book. This never appeared.

Late 1920's: Italian aristocrat and medium Count Centurione Scotto make's gramophone recordings at Millesimo Castle of the 'direct voice'. The Count had contracted the gift seemingly by 'psychic contagion' from the controversial Valiantine.

1928: Thomas Edison worked on equipment he hoped would permit communication with the dead, using a chemical apparatus with potassium permanganate.

1930`s: The Scandinavian military pick up what was probably the first ever polygot messages. These were thought to be stray Nazi transmissions and came to their peak in March 1934 then ceased abruptly. But after the war, when archives searched, no evidence of German involvement was found.

1936: Attilz Von Szalay started to experiment with a Pack-Bell record-cutter and player, trying to capture paranormal voices on phonograph records. Also a ham radio operator Gordon Cosgrave in London apparently picks up Morse code messages between the 'Titanic' and the 'Carpathia' which would have been sent 24 years earlier in 1912 when the 'Carpathia' was racing to the rescue of the stricken 'Titanic'.

1950: John Otto, patent engineer and radio ham together with a group of local radio amateurs in Chicago, USA detects unusual signals of unknown origin on undisclosed frequencies. Lyrical voices using what we now know as polyglot (a mixture of languages) sing and speak in rapid bursts which the group recognized were unlike anything transmitted by regular sources.

Early 1950's: An 'Electronic Communication Society' is formed in Manchester, England where serious attempts are made to amplify by electronic means the pervading energies of the séance room. George Hunt Williamson, author of *"Other Tongues - Other Flesh"* reports of intrusive voices of unknown origin on tape while another American John Keel, investigating UFO reports worldwide, comes up with dozens of reports of voice intrusion culled from military and civilian sources. In his book *"Our Haunted Planet"*, Keel devotes an entire chapter to these rogue transmissions.

1952 Italy: Two Catholic priests, Father Ernetti and Father Gemelli, were collaborating on music research. Ernetti was an internationally respected scientist, a physicist and philosopher, and also a music lover. Gemelli was President of the Papal Academy. On September 15, 1952, while Gemelli and Ernetti were recording a Gregorian chant, a wire on their magnetophone kept breaking. Exasperated, Father Gemelli looked up and asked his father for help. To the two men's amazement, his father's voice, recorded on the magnetophone, answered, "Of course I shall help you. I'm always with you."

They repeated the experiment, and this time a very clear voice filled with humor said, "But Zucchini, it is clear, don't you know it is I?"

Father Gemelli stared at the tape. No one knew the nickname his father had teased him with when he was a boy. He realized then that he was truly speaking with his father. Although his joy at his father's apparent survival was mixed with fear, did he have any right to speak with the dead?

Eventually the two men visited Pope Pius XII in Rome. Father Gemelli, deeply troubled, told the Pope of the experience. To his surprise the Pope patted his shoulder and said, "Dear Father Gemelli, you really need not worry about this. The existence of this voice is strictly a scientific fact and has nothing whatsoever to do with spiritism. The recorder is totally objective. It receives and records only sound waves from wherever they come. This experiment may perhaps become the cornerstone for a building for scientific studies which will strengthen people's faith in a hereafter."

The good father was somewhat reassured. But he made certain that the experiment did not go public until the last years of his life. It wasn't until 1990 that the results were published.

1956: Hollywood, USA photographer and independent voice medium Attila Von Szalay and a psychologist named Raymond Bayless record voices on magnetic tape that should not have been there. Von Szalay had been experimenting since 1947 with phonograph discs and wire recorders and had succeeded in capturing faint whispers. They named the voices they captured 'aerial' voices and reported their discovery in the Journal of the American Society for Psychical Research.

1959: In July of this year Russian born Sir Friedrich Jurgenson, an artist and film producer, records his mother's voice using a reel-to-reel tape recorder at his estate in Mölnbo, Sweden. She had died four years earlier. He went on to record thousands of discarnate voices and is regarded as the 'father' of the EVP.

1964: Jurgenson after 5 years of research publishes his findings in his book Roesterna Fraen Rymden (Voices from the Universe). Attilz Von Szalay gets voices of his deceased relatives on tape for the first time.

1965: A well-known Latvian Philosopher and Psychologist, author of six books Dr. Konstantin Raudive, hears of Jurgenson's work. He had long been interested in the direct voice physical type of mediumship which may have begun in his early post-graduate days at Edinburgh University in 1934.

He meets Jurgenson and sets up his own research project in Germany initially using an ordinary crystal set, the 'cat's whisker' of earlier radio days. Later he enlists the help of Friedberg Karger, a research physicist at the Max Planck Institute in Munich and other electronic engineers. Theodor Rudolph a high-frequency electronics engineer of the well-known firm Telefunken designs an instrument called a 'goniometer' for him. Dr. Raudive eventually records over 100,000 discarnate voices.

Konstantin Raudive's book, *"Breakthrough"* is the catalyst for many of today's researchers.

1967: Thomas Edison spoke through West German clairvoyant Sigrun Seuterman, in trance, about his earlier efforts in 1928 to develop equipment for recording voices from the beyond. Edison also made suggestions as to how to modify TV sets and tune them to 740 megahertz to get paranormal effects. (Session recorded on tape by

Paul Affolter, Liestal, Switzerland). Franz Seidi, Vienna, developed the "sychophone"..

1968: Father Leo Schmid, Oeschgen, Switzerland, was assigned a small parish, to give him time to experiment with taping voices. His book, *"Wen Die Toten Reden" (When the Dead Speak)* was published in 1976, shortly after his death. Raudive published his book *"Unhoerbares Wird Hoerbar" (The Inaudible Becomes Audible)*, based on 72,000 voices he recorded.

1970: D. Scott Rogo and Raymond Bayless publish *"Phone Calls from the Dead"*. Raymond Cass begins experimenting.

1971: Colin Smythe, Ltd. England, published explained English translations of Raudive's book: *"Breakthrough, an Amazing Experiment in Electronic Communication with the Dead"*. Marcello Bacci and his co-workers in Grosseto, Italy made weekly contact with spirit communicators, which still continued in 1988. William Adams Welch publishes his findings *"Talks with the Dead"*. Americans Paul Jones, George W Meek and Hans Heckman, opened a laboratory. This is the to establish the first serious research to create a two-way voice communication system far more sophisticated than the equipment used in EVP approach.

1972: George Gilbert Bonner from England, a psychologist and artist, using a reel-to-reel recorder and battery radio tuned to mush or white noise to act as a carrier for discarnate voices and begins to experiment after reading Dr. Raudive's book. He asks into his microphone: "Can anyone hear me and would anyone like to speak to me?" not expecting any response. He received the answer in a hiss and rush of sound, "Yes". Bonner went on to record more than 50,000 spirit voices over the next 22 years.

At about the same time Raymond Cass, a hearing-aid practitioner in England begins research into EVP using a small battery-operated radio tuned in to 'white noise'. He recorded thousands of clear discarnate voices over the years, speaking and singing, and theorizes that his proximity to a Mass X-Ray unit only 30 yards away produced an emanation which was 'beating' with the selected air band frequency and producing a transient condition enabling the voices to manifest.

1973: Joseph and Michael Lamoreaux, Washington State, had success with recording paranormal voices after reading Raudive's book.

1975: Formation of V.T.F German research group. William Addams Welch, Hollywood script writer and playwright, authored *"Talks with the Dead."*

1978: William O'Neil working for George Meek, using a modified side-band radio had brief, but evidential contact with an American medical doctor said to have died five years earlier.

1981: Manfred Boden has unsolicited contact with communicators of non-human evolution via telephone
and computer.

1982: George Meek (developer of the Spiricom) publishes his results and continues his research with a battery of radio oscillators. Electronics engineer Hans-Otto Koenig helps Radio Luxembourg broadcast live what was claimed to be a two-way conversation with a dead person. Koenig uses an ultrasound device after closely following Meek's work. The equipment is set up under the supervision of the radio station's engineers, connected to a set of speakers, and switched on. After a few seconds a clear voice is heard to saying "Otto Koenig makes wireless with the dead".

George Meek also made a trip around the world to distribute tape recordings of 16 excerpts of communications between William O'Neil and an American scientist who died 14 years earlier. He also distributed a 100-page technical report giving wiring diagrams, photos, technical data and guidelines for research by others. Hans Otto Koenig, West Germany, develops sophisticated electronic equipment, using extremely low beat frequency oscillators, ultra-violet and infra-red lights, etc. Sarah Estep begins the American Association of EVP (AA-EVP)

Also during this time, a discovery was made in 1982 by the three Italian scientists: Roberto Benzi, Alfonso Sutera and Angelo Vulpiani, which found that a background of white noise (or Gaussian noise) was conducive to EVP results. The trio published their findings in the August 1995 issue of the *Scientific American;* the phenomenon which has been described as stochastic resonance (SR). Stochastic resonance can be used to measure transmittance amplitudes below an instrument's detection limit.

1984: Kenneth Webster, England, receives (via several different computers) 250 communications from a person who lived in the 16th century. Most print-outs are in English text consistent with speech at that point in history, and personal details fully supported by library research. Communications are often concurrent with poltergeist-type phenomena. Webster writes book, *"The Vertical Plane"*, with extensive photo documentation in 1989.

1985: Klaus Schreiber, West Germany, with technical assistance from Martin Wenzel, begins to get images of dead persons on TV picture tubes, using opto-electronic feedback systems. There is positive identification in many cases by accompanying audio communications, including audio-video contact with Schreiber's two deceased wives. This work is the subject of a documentary TV film and a book by Rainer Hobbe of Radio Luxembourg.

1986: Jules and Maggie Harsh-Fischbach, Luxembourg, develop and operate two electronic systems superior to that of any of the EVP equipment up to this time.

Swiss electronics engineer Klaus Schreiber gets pictures of the dead on TV. by means of an apparatus he calls 'Vidicom' which consists of a specially adapted TV switched on but not attached to an aerial with a video camera in front of it to capture images that appear on the screen. The word ITC is coined (Instrumental TransCommunication).

1987: The C.E.T.L group formed, Luxembourg.

1989: Samuel Alsop publishes his book, *"Whispers of Immortality."*

1994: Hans Otto Koenig manufactures a Field Generator to communicate with the dead who he claims oscillate on a width frequency of 5 KHz.

1995: INIT formed (International Network for Instrumental TransCommunication, ITC)

2003: Scottish researcher Alexander MacRae made a number of attempts to capture EVP in a specially designed laboratory belonging to the Institute of Noetic Science, Petaluma, California. The laboratory was described as being "double-screened"; shielded against electromagnetic radiation; to prevent interference from radio transmissions or nearby electronic devices, and insulated against sound; to prevent contamination of recordings by external noise sources.

Over the course of the experiment, MacRae reported capturing a number of anomalies which were subsequently isolated and analyzed. Based on this analysis, and the level of screening against outside interference, MacRae concluded that the anomalies represented distinct speech from a source that could not be explained through conventional means.

EVP Today : EVP has moved on somewhat from the image of a researcher sitting in front of a reel to reel tape recorder for hours on end waiting for a disembodied voice to break through. The digital age is upon us and technology is providing us with many more options by which to conduct our experiments.

To date, EVP experiments all over the world have produced far more evidence of an afterlife than any other aspect of paranormal research.

4. Electronic Voice Phenomenon – EVP

What is EVP?

Electronic Voice Phenomena known as EVP is either a sound or a voice which can be recorded onto a variety of recording devices. These voices have been recorded for many years and under a variety of different circumstances. What you are doing as a researcher is building upon the knowledge base as to what these voices and sounds may be, and if we can determine how they are recorded.

Types of EVPs:

Class A - Loud & clear - interpreted the same by all listeners without the need for hearing devices (headphones).

Class B - Reasonably clear - interpreted differently by some listeners many time requiring the use of a listening device.

Class C - Requires headphones to distinguish the voices and open to individual interpretation. With this class of an EVP - I would just enhance the volume if needed and explain to the client that I cannot make a determination as to what is being said. This may be something that they can hear and understand without our help.

Whenever you are going to use software to modify the EVP, make sure you only enhance the volume or try to only eliminate some of the static that may have been recorded. If you need to keep working on an EVP to make it stand out then you have modified too far and it is basically a manufactured EVP.

For clarity you should always indicate in your report what you believe is being said, leaving open the opportunity for your client to make their own interpretation.

How Does an EVP occur?

There is much speculation on how this phenomenon occurs. I can attest to some experimentation that I have done with multiple recorders in different scenarios. What I have noticed is there is no true pattern to how they get recorded and when they get recorded. I have placed as many as 8 recorders in a circle no greater than 2 foot in diameter and have had only 1 of the recorders actually record an EVP.

Why that happens is what we are trying to figure out. Based on seeing this first hand and many similar experiments with the same outcome, I believe that the EVP is imprinted onto the device as opposed to simply recorded onto it. If it was recording the voice then the others should also have recorded it as well, correct?

Who are these spirits or entities we are communicating with?

That is the major question we are trying to answer. Could this actually be Aunt Emma or is it the devil himself pretending to be Aunt Emma? We do not know the answer to that question just yet. We think we are communicating whatever entity that we believe to be occupying the location we are in. We hope it is Aunt Emma, but in reality there is no true way established yet to make that determination.

One thing that is occurring is an energy exchange of some sort between the investigator and the spirit during these communications. This is a type of exchange that both parties need to be open to. If you are in a location and just sit around with an attitude of, "Why am I here?" I can almost promise that you will not record any EVP's.

If, instead, you are in a good frame of mind that is open to this energy exchange then an EVP may come from it.

Normally, the investigator is unaware of his or her part in this transfer of information. The attitude and desire of the researcher is a critical component to allow this exchange of energy to be successful.

Around the world people have been recording for years, so why is it that sometimes an American investigator, while in Germany, will record an English EVP? This lends some credence to the fact that the investigator is an important conduit for this energy exchange to occur rather than the only English speaking spirit found him while he was over there.

What does all this mean? Basically if an entity wants to communicate, they must find a way to bring their words into our reality. The investigator provides the medium (voice recorder) and the channel for that communication exchange to take place. This may not work for you the first time out or even the second time out, so just keep on trying and one day you may have the best evidence ever recorded.

EVP Equipment:

The basic equipment that you would need to be efficient with EVP would be a digital voice recorder, computer and analyzing software. I would also suggest noise reducing head phones. This is the basics to get started. Most of which are inexpensive and easily available at several store chains.

Several people prefer to use a cassette recorder. There is no problem with doing so but you need to be aware of a few things if you decide to go this route. Always use a new tape when you are doing EVP work. This way you can guarantee that there is no cross contamination from a previous recording.

There are several versions of this style recorder available and you may also notice you can record the mechanism working inside the recorder. To help eliminate this problem you should use an external microphone. A small omni-directional microphone is an inexpensive solution for this and you should be able to pick one up wherever you purchased your recorder.

I do suggest that you find an acceptable sound editing program and learn to work with it. This type of program is a good tool for slightly manipulating your EVP's and for cutting them down into smaller manageable files. Whenever you use these programs, you should never overwork the recording or you may end up with an EVP that sounds manufactured and that is not a good piece of evidence. When working with these programs never work directly with the original recording, always work on a copy. This way you have a back-up.

Uploading your recordings:

I suggest, until you are accustomed to your recorder that you upload the entire recording for review. You can always cut out the appropriate sections at a later time. Begin by preparing to play the recorder, while at the same time preparing to start the recording on the software. Typically there is a red button that says "record". Start playing the recorder and press "record" simultaneously, this will now record onto your computer.

It's important to keep a log of the times for all of your recordings. You must either verbalize the time at the beginning of each recording or you must have a recorder that log's the time for you. I have the latter and it makes life so much easier. You are now ready to review your recordings.

Many of today's recorders will already come with software for downloading onto your computer. I have a several digital voice recorders from various manufacturers that all came with software and I still use these recorders for my primary EVP recording devices. Other style of recorders required a patch cord to be used for uploading to your computer. This is a cord found at most electronic supply stores.

How to use a patch cord:

This is for those of you that have an older style recorder. Your computer must be ready to accept audio from your line-in jack. Click on the volume horn on your computer screen. The location will vary from computer to computer but most are adjacent to your digital clock in your status bar. Double click on the horn, then click "options" then select "properties". In this window, click on "recording" and make sure you have the "Line-in" box checked, and then press "OK".

You now can adjust the volume for the "Line-in". You will want to set it to a level in which you can to hear everything clearly. Plug one end of the patch cord into the "Ear/ Headphone" jack on your recording device and plug the opposite end into the "Line-in" jack of your computers sound card. You are now connected and ready to upload.

You will now need to open the software with which you will be reviewing the recordings. The following will vary slightly depending on your recording software but the principles are the same. For the beginner we will set the software to record in mono at 16 bit. It's now time to upload your recordings.

Reviewing your recordings:

You should download your recordings using the software that came with the recorder. Helpful tip: I personally keep my entire investigation log on this recorder, so when I start the play back I begin to write my report as well. When you think you may have captured an EVP, on a separate piece of paper, mark down the section of the recording, indicating recording number and at what time during the recording you believe something may have been imprinted.

After the initial review of all the recordings, it is time to go back into the sections where there are possible EVP's. At this point, I have the head phones ready if needed. When you come across a section which may contain an EVP, you may need to convert the file format into another that is compatible with your editing software. This is the time to do that, and remember always keep the original.

So, now you have what you consider to be a possible EVP. You have clearly labeled your new file and you have indicated in your report that this piece of "potential" evidence exists. You can remove it from your report later if it is not an EVP. Now you can clip it down into a manageable segment. If you asked a question and received an immediate response, I think it is a good idea to leave your voice asking the question with the actual EVP. This way everyone can understand the context of the EVP and also gives the client and others the ability to do their own voice comparison if they so choose.

Techniques for recording:

This will vary for each person, especially as you develop your own style. Typically when doing an EVP recording session, I like to minimize the length of my recordings. This is because you must review all of your recordings in order to properly investigate. If you have recorded for three or more hours, then you need to listen carefully for three or more hours. The average amount of recording time I would go for during a three hour investigation is approximately forty-five minutes to an hour and this includes notes concerning the investigation.

When you do an EVP session, be prepared to ask a series of questions and allow a minimum of 10 seconds between questions for an answer to be recorded. Keep these sessions to approximately 30-60 second intervals. This way you have a manageable amount of recordings to review and you also have a stopping point if needed during review, and believe me after a while you will need that stopping point.

This now leads into what to ask during a typical EVP session. This also will vary from investigator to investigator. Just remember to not ask an open ended question. That means don't ask, "Can you make a noise for us?"

What happens if the noise is a sonic boom next to your ear? That wouldn't be good for anyone. If you want to ask for a noise be specific. "Can you knock gently on the table if you want to talk to us?"

EVP's will occur wherever and whenever they wish. I have gathered many EVP's just from when I was making notes about the investigation or speaking with the client. So please carefully review all of your recordings.

Electronic Voice Phenomena - Questions to Ask:

There is no right or wrong questions to ask. If you have a "feeling" that you are dealing with a child, or an older woman than ask a question that you feel they can relate to. If you are in a location with a known history, i.e. Gettysburg, ask questions pertaining to that time in history.

The more specific you can be the better. It is also great to try and mix it up. As an investigator, you can get bored with the same monotonous questions time after time. Another approach to try is to ask the same question in different ways. This method is used to help verify that you are truly communicating with a spirit and not picking up on any random radio or TV signals.

As you get started, explain out loud what you are going to do. This will let whoever is in the room with you know that you have a recording device which can capture their voice if they choose to speak into it. Point out the location of where the microphone is and ask the spirit to speak loudly and clearly. Tell them you may not hear them while you are sitting there but could hear them later if they speak into the device. If you are planning on a second trip to the location you are in, tell the spirits that you may be able to provide an answer to their questions when you return.

Now it's time to start asking your questions. After you ask one question, give some time to allow for an answer; allow a minimum of 10. The number of questions you ask is a personal preference. Just remember the more you ask the more you will have to review.

Be comfortable and relaxed while doing an EVP session. You are a conduit through which the phenomena will take place. If you are not in the right frame of mind, allow others to ask the questions and record along. Attitude is very important during an EVP session.

One last thing to mention about the recording of EVP's, we have noticed in the past that when conversations are occurring between investigators you may be able to get someone else chiming in. So we have gotten ourselves into the habit of turning on our recorders during our conversations while on an investigation. You never know.

Below is a list of some generic questions that you can use when you are just getting started:
- Is there anyone here that would like to talk with us?
- What is your name?
- How old are you?
- Was this your home?
- Can you see us?
- How many of us do you see?
- What color are your eyes?
- Do you have a favorite color?

At the completion of your recording session always be courteous, remember ghosts were people too and if you are respectful of them they may be more open to communicating with you.

Some tips on using a digital voice recorder:
- Have everyone present say their name into your recorder so you have a voice comparison for later just in case you're not sure if someone in the group spoke during your recording.
- Verify that your recorder does have a time stamp capability. If it does not just look at your watch and state the time whenever you make a note or start an EVP session.
- Never use voice activation mode, this can turn on a little late and you can miss an important piece of evidence.
- Always speak in a normal tone, do not whisper. Whenever you do or someone in your group does it can make you think you have a false positive EVP.
- Make notes during an EVP session when something occurs so you are not thinking later that it was an anomalous event.
  - Car passing by
  - Sirens outside
  - Someone walking around in your group
  - Someone whispering
  - Meters going off
  - Other members in different locations making any noises or talking.

- ○ Weather noises affecting the location
    - Rattling windows
    - Trees brushing against a window
    - Rain
    - Thunder
    - Doors opening and closing

Finally if you are in a location where voices can carry, or movement from other team members can easily be heard from where you are, be sure to ask your team members to properly allow you time to record. Letting others know they can be heard will eliminate unwanted noise when you review your recorded session. It's also a good idea to let others in the room know when you are about to start a recording session, so they can record along with you. You never know who will pick up an EVP.

A great resource for EVP is the American Association of Electronic Voice Phenomenon (aaevp.) They are many articles to help you learn more about EVP on their website at www.aaevp.com

5. Photography 101 for the Investigator

Let's face it; the days of film (35 MM) are pretty much over with. This is a good thing because now we don't have to spend all of that money on film development! The second positive that came from this technology trend is that more photos are being taken which increases the likely hood of capturing something anomalous with your camera.

We now have a larger volume of photos for every investigation. Before it was common to go out and only use two maybe three rolls of film which would yield maybe a little over one hundred photos per group. Today each investigator typically takes hundreds of photos themselves. The odds are in your favor of capturing something interesting with the more photographs taken, so take multiple photos.

Understanding your camera:

Today most investigators are using simple digital cameras which are relatively inexpensive. I suggest that you utilize a camera with as high a resolution as you can. In other words a 10 megapixel camera is better than a 5 megapixel camera. The better the definition of a photo the less likely you are to call something paranormal that is not paranormal.

The number of potential paranormal photos has risen exponentially over the years and many are asking why. One of the first reasons is that the digital camera can view the infrared light spectrum which is invisible to the naked eye. A simple test is to look at the business end of your TV remote control while pressing any button. You will not see anything, but now do this same thing while looking at the view thru your digital camera and you will see the IR lights that are sent out from your remote control.

Digital cameras also allow us the ability to take a large number of photos instead of the old film processing cost/method. Utilize a memory card that gives you the benefit of storing quite a few photos. Obviously the size of the photos (megapixel) will also determine the number of photos being stored, so if you have a high megapixel camera, 10 or higher, you may want to make sure you utilize a 10 gig memory card that is suitable for your camera,

One of the most obvious benefits of a digital camera is utilizing the instant review feature. You can see if you are capturing any evidence and continue to focus on those areas where you do.

All digital cameras utilize optical enhancements to process the photo you have taken; this could be something as basic as red eye reduction. Through some of these enhancements there can be some malfunctions that occur, light can be misread or pixels can get taken away all causing false positive photos.

The location of the flash is another culprit of false positive photos. With today's digital cameras the distance between the lens and the built-in flash has decreased, thereby decreasing the angle of light reflection to the lens. That means that you are more than likely to pick up a reflection off a small, before invisible to the naked eye, particle. The closer the flash is to the lens of the camera the greater the possibility of light reflecting form a drop of moisture or a piece of dust. This is referred to as backscatter.

If you know someone that has a digital SLR camera, it's a good idea to do some experimental work with them. Each of you should take photos in the same areas under the same conditions. You will most likely see the smaller camera with the flash close to the lens will produce more 'orbs' or false positive photos. The reason this doesn't happen with the SLR is the position of the flash to the lens, it is separated and placed on the top of the camera. Often investigators will utilize an extension boot to move the flash even further away to help eliminate these problems.

So now you have the camera and you are going to use whichever one it is on your investigations, what should you do first? Well take as many photos in as many different conditions and light levels as you can. Create a dust storm by banging some of your couch pillows together and start to photograph the dust.

Take photos outdoors in all weather conditions and photograph your breath when it is cold out. Take photos of pollen and bugs at night and during the day and study how they appear in your camera. Many of today's "angel" photos are just photos of bugs spreading their wings. Try to do all of this is as many different light levels as possible.

This will give you a reference library of how your camera reacts under different conditions then you can always refer back to them when you believe you have photographed a paranormal anomaly. Most importantly study the photos you have taken for your reference library. You want to know what to look for that is different from these photos and then you may have something.

If you think you have caught something unusual, be as skeptical as possible. Never assume an anomaly as being something paranormal. Look for all possible explanations and try to replicate the shot. This is your best approach. If you can replicate the shot more than likely you are not dealing with the paranormal.

Another aspect that many people overlook when utilizing the digital camera is the shutter speed. You want to set this as low as you can. If you leave it open for just 1 second you can and will have those streaks you see on many websites. You can also easily take a photo of an apparition this way. Set your camera in a stationary location and set it to take a photograph you. Just as the flash occurs immediately start to walk out of the frame. You will be left with what looks similar to an apparition. So once again study your camera and properly set the shutter speed.

As human beings we tend to look for familiar shapes in a collection of objects, this is known as Matrixing. If you notice when you take a photo of a fully developed tree, many people will start to see faces in the shapes of the leaves and the light pockets, this is also known as a condition called pareidolia or apophenia. This is normal and as an investigator you need to understand that this could be happening during your review.

How to take a photo:

Make sure you note any potential items that could lead to a false positive photo. Street lights, mirrors and other reflective surfaces. In public buildings make sure you note the exit signs, these are on emergency power and will always be on. Watch for dust or dirt being stirred up. Clean your lens (this may seem like a 'duh', but you'd be surprised how many people forget.)

Catching ectoplasmic mist photos can be a great piece of evidence as are vortices, so let's try to eliminate all potentially false positive photos by not smoking and watching your breath in the winter months.

- Make sure you clean your camera's lens regularly throughout the investigation; you could inadvertently touch the cameras lens while you are walking around.
- If your hair is long it should be tied back neatly, it's those single hairs that get photographed all of the time and sent in saying look I found a vortex!
- Make sure your camera is utilizing new batteries or it is fully charge.
- The memory card should be empty and ready for a new investigation
- Remove your camera strap if possible, if you cannot, secure it in your hand or over your wrist. If there is the potential for the strap to get in front of the lens you will be forced to discount the photo.
- Watch where you have placed your fingers. You will get some pretty cool photos when your finger is slightly over the flash or in the lens so be careful.
- Weather conditions are very important for doing spirit photography. Cold and humid air are the primary culprits by indicating you breath in the cold and by water vapor being present in your shots in humid conditions.
  - Hold your breath for a second before and after each photo.
- Make sure you have noted all reflective surfaces from your walk through

When do I take a photo?

There are several instances when you should be taking photos and they start the moment after you arrived on site. Here are some key times to take a photo:
- During the initial walk thru of the location, take several photos of each room looking in all directions. If possible do a 360 view including floor and ceiling. This will show you where everything is at and give you a point of reference if needed during your investigation. It will also indicate reflective surfaces which you need to be aware of during your investigation.

- If you do a "lights out" investigation, take another series of photos when you start investigating, again for point of reference and view in a different light setting.
- If there is any possible activity that has occurred, i.e. a knocking sound or a door opening take several photos.
- If any of your equipment indicates something just occurred take several photos. Here is where several investigators make a simple mistake. Don't just photograph the device which recorded the anomaly but the area around it and around the entire room, remember that spirits move.
- If someone you are with says they feel something
- If you have the urge to just take a photo, do so. Maybe something is telling you they are here to say hello.
- It is also a good idea to take another panoramic shot of the room you're in when you leave, this way you may have something in a different position than when you started that you didn't see move while you were in there.
- Use your senses, if you smell, hear or taste something that doesn't make sense to you, take a series of photos.
- Ask any potential spirits if you can take their photo. Indicate an area for them to stand or sit and do a minor countdown 3,2,1, flash and then say thank you. You never know but it's worth a shot.
- Take as many photos as possible.

Photo evaluation 101:

One of the most difficult tasks we will do as paranormal investigators is review photographic evidence. To properly review our photo's we need to be open-minded but at the same time have a skeptic's eye. This type of evidence is open to interpretation so we need to be very clear on how we define a positive photo, our reputation depends on it.

We have to be strict in our evaluation of photos so that if there is any doubt of what the photo contains, we must put it aside as an unusable photo. Quite often these unusable photos are positive ones but for various reasons we cannot use it as evidence in a case. For example: you have taken a photo and it has an apparition in it, but you took the photo directly at a mirror and the reflection of the flash now makes it possible for a variety of light effects to have occurred. This now makes the photo unusable, it stink's but we can't use it.

What is an Orb?

Orbs are believed to be balls of energy that are visible in the area of light between visible light and the infrared light spectrum. It is a common belief in the field that an orb "could" represent the start of spirit manifestation; orbs are a hot topic of discussion within the investigative field.

A true orb is perfectly round and could be emitting a light. Sometimes we just see the outer edge of these orbs. Orbs are everywhere, take a photo right now in your living room and you may find one. Does this mean Uncle Harry has stopped in for a visit? Maybe or maybe not. We are trying to determine exactly what these orbs may be with our investigations.

We do know that orbs are everywhere, but they have been documented in higher concentration in a known haunted location. The average amount of orb photos in most locations is approximately 5-6%. This is why we ask for the number of photos taken by you on an investigation report. When we do the final report we list the total number of photos taken versus the positive photos obtained and come along with our percentage. If we are above the 6% number then that is a good indication of something occurring there.

How do we tell an orb from dust?

Believe it or not this really isn't that difficult, but it does depend on how you view your photos.

- Never make a determination of a positive photo by looking at it through your camera.
- Always view your photos on your computer at the highest resolution you can.
- When you see what could be an orb slowly zoom into it and look closely at it. Examine at the shape; is it truly round in shape or are there any deviations in the circumference? Does it look slightly oval? If so then these are dust particles, which look very similar to orbs. They sometimes appear as full and the

44

bounce reflection of your flash gives it the appearance it has a light emanating from it.

If you produce an orb photo and say, "look it has a face in it". That is definitely dust. As human beings we are prewired to interpret images into faces etc. (this is a well-documented psychological phenomenon known as *paradolia*).

Think about a time as a child when you looked up at the big fluffy clouds and would see a face, also how many pairs of socks out there has the face of Lincoln? It is a survival mechanism resident in our primitive brain. As an investigator we need be aware of this. Understand and look further into all possibilities.

Let's try an experiment. The easiest way to consider this is to hold up a ball, even take a photo of a ball thrown in the air. Take many different photos from many different angles. You will notice the consistency; the ball is the same shape in every photo and every angle. When we describe orbs we describe them as "balls of energy", so the ball experiment will prove to you the shape doesn't distort from any angle.

If you want to practice at looking at this, get out your camera and get a couch pillow or something similar and bang it with something. Immediately start taking photos, this is dust but when you first look it will appear to be a group of orbs. Look closely at them on your computer and you will start to see the deviations I'm talking about.

The Orb Phenomenon – Is it or isn't it paranormal?

There has been a lot of discussion and speculation in recent years on orbs. Research shows there are three possible explanations for orbs:

Let me start with a brief story on why I believe there to be some credence to orbs. I have personally seen some compelling evidence on orbs which makes me not want to dismiss them across the board. I have seen orbs transition into an apparition. This particular occurrence was being filmed with infrared cameras but they recording was not clear. Another person witnessed this phenomenon along side of me but it is just more anecdotal evidence now. The sad part of this is that it is now just a story. Hopefully as time goes on, others may also see something similar for themselves.

We had been investigating a well documented haunted museum. We were in a bedroom display of the former owner, which is normally roped off to the public. We had noticed when viewed through our video equipment the orbs were not present except for when one particular investigator entered this one room.

We tried to replicate the orbs we witnessed by shaking the pillows and disturbing the rugs, all to no avail. We sent in this investigator and asked him to stand next to the camera. All of a sudden, an orb storm began. We had been positioned outside of the room and could clearly see inside the room, both through the TV cameras and with our own eyes. As we were watching we began to ask the former owner to come to the camera and show us his face.

Almost immediately an orb approached the camera and began to expand, to a point where we could start to make out a body and the formation of a face. As quickly as it started, it dissipated. Immediately we went and rewound the tape. When viewed it looked like a fresh new tape that had never been recorded on, useless but we had a story. We saw an orb start to transition into a form. This was an orb that was only seen with an IR camera. I have another similar account but we will save that for another time.

What is this phenomenon? Is it just the backscatter of your camera or is it possibly something more. How do you explain the orb's that are viewed in the IR light spectrum? We all know that walking around can produce orbs and that we should never take photo in rain, snow, fog or high humidity.

But aren't we trying to be as scientific as possible when doing our research? If you are going to an investigation and you're doing any of these things then you need to find something else to do. You are creating a contaminant in an area which you are controlling as much as possible, the environment. I believe the "orb" discussion needs to be categorized to get a better understanding of everything that has been said or could be said. By that I mean who is making the statement on what the anomaly is.

I believe there are three categories that need to be assigned to groups and individuals that are looking at and quantifying these photographs and they are:

- Scientific Researchers – Those that use a scientific approach to research and have an understanding of what could cause these photographic anomalies.
- Hobbyist – These are the individuals or groups that get together after reading one or two web sites and decide they will make their judgment and that is what it will be. They don't completely understand what else could be the cause of these anomalies.
- Pure skeptic – These are the people that no matter what you say or how you say it will not believe anything but their point of view.

What else should we consider? Yes it is believed that spirit manifestation begins within the invisible infrared light spectrum. Many did not realize at the time when they came out, but digital cameras can see into this light spectrum. We can correlate the "rise" of orb photos to the inception of looking into a previously invisible spectrum of light which the normal researcher could not view before. Does this mean now that orbs are paranormal? Absolutely not, but does it now create a possibility that they could be? Let's not forget we can also attribute many to the backscatter due to the flash/lens proximity.

Many researchers that keep track of what they do and how they do it can confirm some of what I am going to say here. First is that we all know we will capture some form of "orb" photography on an investigation. Does this make it paranormal, once again the answer is no. But if you start to correlate all you are doing you may see some interesting findings that you didn't look at before. Most serious investigators keep track of everything, what time did this occur, weather conditions, etc. Many even keep track of how many photos they have taken. This is an important number and I will explain why in a minute.

We all know there are documented haunted locations, non-haunted locations and those we need to yet look into. Researcher that keep track of their photos along with the locations may see some interesting things. You may notice that the "orb" phenomenon occurs in a higher concentration in a known haunted location. We all know we will see orbs when we take our photos, but why is it that they are in a higher concentration in a known haunted location?

On average you may see a number of 4% of your photos containing some orb manifestation. But in a known haunt ,that number can rise to 5, 6 or even 10% of photos having orbs. Does this mean that the location has a bad house keeper? Or that the investigator is running around causing these dust storms? Once again if you are in control you can answer those questions, however for the prudent investigator that leaves the question of why are there more in these locations?

Should I just submit an orb photo as evidence alone? Within in our group there are many thoughts on orbs; most do not agree they are anything paranormal. That also doesn't mean they are not. We try to maintain an open mind when reviewing them.

Don't get me wrong, this is not an affirmation saying all orbs are paranormal, this is just saying what about these other facts. As scientific researchers move on in this field we have to remember we cannot throw out all of the possibilities yet. We are learning and have to keep an open mind to all possibilities. Keep track of what is occurring on your investigations, keep track of your numbers and start to formulate your own catalog of information. Reading what others have to say is a great start, but your own research must be done to properly formulate your opinion.

Just remember there is more that we do not know out there. We are in this field to study and advance it. Until we can say and prove without a doubt that orbs are just dust we still must keep an open mind to what they could be.

Why some photos that are partially blurred out considered good?

There many photos, some clear and others not so clear that say they are true apparition photos. Are they? Well that is also open to interpretation. I have been onsite when apparition photos were taken and I have seen many photos that claim to be apparition photos. The ones that I have seen personally and have been witness to by people I respect, all have the same style of image in them, and that is they are focused throughout the shot but where the apparition is located it appears blurry and a bit out of focus. Ten years ago we would say it was a developing error, but we can't say that with today's digital technology. The blurred apparition is most likely due to the shutter speed being set too high, greater than a second.

Vortex: A vortex is believed to be a spot where spirits pass from one plane to another. This is an anomaly that we can photograph. The problem with this is that it does look like a camera strap or hair so we need to be sure where the camera strap is at the time of a photograph.

Light rods: Typically in our field when we photograph light rods they are actually orbs moving at a high speed. They will appear as streaks in your photo. Hair could also give you the same impression so put your hair back.

Ectoplasm Mist: As stated earlier this is a great piece of evidence to obtain. The problem is the potential for outside influence. Watch your breath in cold temperatures, no smoking, lookout for candles, fire places, etc anything that may have recently been ignited.

Now how can you tell you have a good photo of ectoplasm mist? If it is your breath there may be a bluish or even brownish tint to it. It will also have some stringy looking vapor to it. If it is cigarette smoke it will have a bluish tint and be stringy as well.

True mist looks like a piece of cotton, a consistent solid cotton piece that is mostly white or grey in color. The start of the mist maybe somewhat stringy so you need to make sure you document what you were doing and where you were.

6. Equipment

This chapter could easily be a separate book itself and for that very reason we will cover some of the basic equipment and what it does along with how it works. There is much more out there than what we will cover so don't start the email campaigns on you didn't talk about this or that. This is my opinion on what the basics are.

The first order is to understand what you are going to use the equipment for and what are you going to need to accomplish that. In later chapters I will discuss a time line so first and foremost you will need a watch, pen and pad of paper. If you are a little more advance you can use a digital voice recorder with a date and time stamp to accomplish the same thing.

The reason I have made this a separate item is because without your timeline you cannot tie any other evidence together that you may get while you are out there.

The main pieces of evidence that you would get on an investigation are in the following forms:

Photos:

In chapter 5 we discussed in detail the cameras and how to properly do spirit photography. Cameras are a piece of equipment that most people already own. Just to reiterate that you should use a 5 mega pixel or greater camera when doing spirit photography. If you are lucky enough to own a SLR camera with a flash extension that would be even better. The further the flash is from the lens the better.

Audio:

Electronic Voice Phenomenon (EVP) is one thing every investigator seems to get excited about. Please refer to chapter 4 for more discussion on EVP. Most investigators utilize digital voice recorders in their investigations. Digital voice recorders vary in price from approximately $35.00 into the hundreds of dollars. Cost is always a factor when starting out but if you can afford to spend from $50.00 to $100.00 for a recorder it is money well spent.

Some people still like to utilize an analog recorder, which is acceptable. If you plan on using one of these devices it is always best to use it in conjunction with an external microphone. The reason for this is that you can record the mechanisms within the device which will make you think that you have some anomalous event recorded. The cost factor comes into play with this device as well. You should always use new tapes whenever you record with this device. If you record over a previous investigation there is a possibility that there will be contamination.

Whichever you decide to go with take the time to get use to working with it. Do experimental recordings in various conditions so you get use to the noise that it will pick up. I have heard a noise on a digital recorder that if I didn't share it with my first director I would have sworn it was the devil himself coming thru. There are times when digital recorders will make an obnoxious noise that you will hear when reviewing your recording, the only way I can describe it is that is sounds like a loud, guttural voice saying "phrump". Now don't let that scare you, if you hear something like that you now know that your digital voice recorder can make that sound.

Hand Held Video:

Many teams today also use hand held video cameras in their investigations. There are some good and bad points to using these devices. If you capture an anomalous event on your video camera you will have a time table indicating the duration of the event. This is great information to put away for your research. The problem I have seen is that many new investigators pull out the family camera to get started. You want to make sure that your camera has a night shot capacity if you plan on going lights out. If not you will have many great hours of blacked out footage to review. More often than not the cameras night shot setting is insufficient for an investigation so you will need to purchase an Infra-red light extender. There are several on the market so you will need to find one that is suitable for your use.

Other than the obvious video you can also record EVP's on your video camera. So whenever you are reviewing this evidence make sure your sound is on. You never know where that voice will appear.

Once again a cost factor comes into play with video cameras as well. You should never record over a used tape or DVD. Always supply new ones for each investigation. You may also consider having a back-up battery for the video recorder. Many times these batteries only last from ½ hour to 1 hour and most investigations run much longer than that.

A tripod is a great accessory that you can use with your camera. You can set-up a camera in a location believed to be very active and continuously record for the entire investigation. When you set this up try to place the camera away from where other investigators would walk in front of it or where there are outside influences on the camera. You want to get a good recording without contamination.

Finally don't forget what time you started to record, you may have to keep track of time to change out your tapes.

Electromagnetic Field Detectors - EMF meters:

The primary point to remember is that most of the equipment used by a paranormal investigator was designed for other fields and has found a home in our field. Be that right or wrong, that's where we are with the equipment. Some are companies are starting to manufacture equipment directly for the paranormal industry; however their primary functions are based on the earlier non-paranormal devices.

There are several models and types of EMF meters on the market today and we could spend the next 100 pages discussing them all. We will stick with some of the more basic models for our discussion. These models are also the most inexpensive ones out there. They range in price from $15.00 up to $200.00. With these various pieces of equipment it is possible to track and locate and both electric and magnetic energy sources. These meters detect fluctuations within the nearby electromagnetic fields as well as low strength moving EMF fields. These are known as ELF or Extremely Low Frequency EMF.

Electromagnetic field meter, (sometimes referred to as an EMF detector) is a scientific instrument for measuring electromagnetic radiation. There are many different types of EMF meters, but the two main categories are single axis and tri-axis. Single axis meters only measures one dimension of the nearby field. Single axis instruments have to be tilted and turned on all three axes to obtain a full measurement. A tri-axis meter measures all three axes simultaneously. Most meters measure the electromagnetic radiation flux density, which is the amplitude of any emitted radiation. Other meters measure the change in an electromagnetic field over time. Electromagnetic fields can be either AC (Alternating current) or DC (Direct current).

An EMF meter can measure AC electromagnetic fields, which are usually emitted from man-made sources such as electrical wiring, while Gauss meters or magnetometers measure DC fields, which occur naturally in the earth's geomagnetic field; and are emitted from other sources where direct current is present. EMF meters usually measure radiation in milligauss. In absence of a moving magnetic field, an ideal meter will read 0 milligauss. Industrial EMF meters will often read 2-3 milligauss when placed in an open field devoid of emitters such as power lines (either overhead or buried). The majority of EMF meters available are calibrated to measure electromagnetic radiation, which is alternating at 50/60Hz (the frequency of US and European mains electricity)This is because in recent years people have become concerned about the long-term health effects of exposure to high levels of radiation emitted from some electrical appliances. There are other meters which can measure field alternating at as little as 20 Hz However these tend to be much more expensive and are only used to specific research.

Most of the meters in use by the paranormal investigators measure in terms of "milligauss". This is a unit of magnetic flux density equal to one-thousandth of a gauss. This is about to get a little more technical so hang on. Magnetic flux is the group of magnetic field lines emitted outward from the north pole of a magnet. Magnetic flux density is the amount of magnetic flux per unit area of a section, perpendicular to the direction of flux. The SI unit of measurement for magnetic flux is the weber (w). The SI unit of measurement for magnetic flux density is weber per square meter which equals a tesla.

What is a Milligauss?

Milligauss is a measurement of electrical current (mg). **milli-** (symbol **m**) is a prefix in the SI and other systems of units denoting a factor of 10^{-3}, or 1/1,000 (one thousandth).A gauss is a unit of magnetic flux density. A gauss is 10-4 Tesla's per square centimeter. And a Milligauss is 1/1000 of that. **What is a tesla?** The **tesla** (symbol

T) is the SI derived unit of magnetic field **B** (which is also known as "magnetic flux density" and "magnetic induction").

One billionth of a tesla is a nanotesla, equivalent to .01 mG or 0.01 milligauss, and it is in nanotesla that common metric home measurements are made to determine local magnetic field exposure. 1 tesla is equivalent to:

- 10,000 (or 10^4) gauss (G), used in the CGS system. Thus, 10 G = 1 mT (1 millitesla)
- 1,000,000,000 (or 10^9) gammas (γ), used in geophysics. Thus, 1 γ = 1 nT (nanotesla)

For those concerned with low-frequency electromagnetic radiation in the home, the following conversions are needed most:

- 1000 nanotesla = 1 microtesla = 10 milligauss (mG)
- 1,000,000 microtesla = 1 tesla
- 200 nanotesla = US Congress and WHO Recommended limit for constant human exposure = 2 mG

Magnetic Flux Density

Magnetic flux density is the amount of magnetic flux per unit area of a section, perpendicular to the direction of flux. A vector quantity measures the strength and direction of the magnetic field around a magnet or an electric current.

Magnetic flux density is equal to magnetic field strength times the magnetic permeability in the region in which the field exists. Electric charges moving through a magnetic field are subject to a force described by the equation $F = qv \times B$, where q is the amount of electric charge, v is the velocity of the charge, B is the magnetic flux density at the position of the charge, and × is the vector product. Magnetic flux density also can be understood as the density of magnetic lines of force, or magnetic flux lines, passing through a specific area. It is measured in units of tesla.

To obtain the proper measurement, it is important that the actual sensor within the EMF meter corresponds to the direction of maximum field strength at any given location. If it does not, then you will risk making measurements that may be much lower than the true field strength. The easiest way to determine the actual measurement is to use a 3-axis meter. This meter does the actual computation for you and you do not need to rotate the meter around the source.

There are many things that have and will give off an electromagnetic field. The earth itself generates these magnetic fields as do all of the following:

- light poles
- electrical outlets
- Computers and monitors
- Printers and routers
- Cell phones (always keep one with you but it should be off)
- Refrigerators'
- Microwaves
- Stoves/range
- Televisions
- VCR/DVD players
- Stereos
- Mechanical equipment – Heaters/AC units

The list can go on and on but these are what you will most likely run across. You should always do a base EMF sweep of a location at the start of the investigation to determine if there are any high EMF areas that will affect your meters.

Electrical wiring and water pipes are a notorious place that can carry high EMF readings. Even if there is no "power" running through the circuit it will still carry a measurable EMF. Wiring over head can have a spike in EMF when a device in the circuit powers on, so do not assume what just happened was paranormal. Yes I did say water pipes! We were in a home that had an EMF reading as high as 135 mg in the basement, where we were able to trace this back to the incoming water services in some older piping.

When using the EMF meters, you are looking for fluctuations of 1.5 to 7.0 milligauss (mg). It is within this range some believe we can measure a spirit presence. Anything higher is typically a man made application or occurrence and lower normally has a natural source, such as the normal earth magnetic north pull.

Electromagnetic fields are directional. The primary field strength is dependent upon the direction of current flow (electric). The field strength will decrease the as it moves further away from the primary source. Picture the ripple effect, the further away the ripple from the center the smaller the ripple will be.

There is no data to support the theory that a ghost or any other form of a spirit emits an EMF. This also means there is no data to say they have the ability to use EMF from a man made or natural sources. A lot of research has been undertaken which strongly suggests that when some people are exposed to a powerful EMF or a less powerful but varying EMF they may report sensations that they may believe are paranormal in origin.

These effects include a sense of presence, a sense of touch, anxiety, unease, fear, nausea and even an 'Out of Body' sensation. These types of sensations can occur if you are exposed to higher levels of EMF. This is why we look at these levels while investigating. If the levels are consistently high then there may be some sensitivity to high EMF from the participants and we need to let them know that we found this in the location.

Commonly Used EMF Meters:

Trifield Natural EMF detector is a 3-axis meter and the most expensive version of the basic meters which we will discuss. It is also the best meter in terms of accuracy and distance covered. This meter is sensitive enough to register a thunder storm as far away as 25 miles. So you do need to be aware of what is "around" you when using this meter.

The meter has an analog readout on the front which works well in a lighted area. It also has an adjustment knob located on the right side of the meter which allows you to set the device to alarm at a certain levels. This is a low audible alarm but one that can be used in the same room you are in. This device can be set to measure electric and magnetic fields separately or set to "SUM" which makes it a true EMF detector. The effective coverage area of this meter is approximately 25 feet.

This meter is extremely sensitive to movement and is best used in a stationary mode. It will settle down once it adjusts to the area it is placed in. After it is properly set just let it be and sit back and do your investigation. When there is a fluctuation in the nearby electromagnetic field at the level you have adjusted it to, there will be an audible alarm. The down side is that you will always need to check the alarm whenever you move the device from location to location. It can also be a little tricky for some people to set properly.

When setting this device place it on a flat surface and start to adjust the knob on the right hand side. You will notice the sound will go off as you turn the knob. Keep track of where that sound is off on the analog read out. You would want to set this meter to go off between 1.5 – 2 mg. If the device has rested too long you will notice you cannot make it alarm, just pick it up and move it around and try to set it again

The Trifield EMF detector requires a 9 volt battery. The battery compartment is on the back of the device and must be removed with a small screw driver to access the compartment (It is also a good idea to have a small toolkit with your gear).

Cell Sensor EMF detector is a single axis style meter that can be used in 2 ways. This is one of my favorite meters because it has both a visual and audible alarm which is easily heard. The base unit can be utilized as a standalone radio frequency (RF) detector; however we always insert the probe that comes with the meter to make it an EMF detector. It comes with a 2 foot long probe that when plugged in the alarm feature is activated. The visual signal is a bright red flashing light of the front end of the meter. There is also an analog display with a needle for reference which is visible with a flash light. They also include a volume control on the side of the meter. The effective range of this meter is approximately10 feet.

This meter can be hand held or stationary. If you are planning on using it as a hand held style do not hold the probe by the wire. I have seen plenty of people walk around, doing just that, but it will give you a false positive reading. I have fashioned Velcro strips to the meter and the probe to prevent the probe wire from being bent. The "business" end of the probe is situated directly below the red light and is easy to walk around with.

When the meter is set-up for EMF detection it registers ELF or Extremely Low Frequency EMF. The gauge on the front of the meter has 2 separate lines for reading the EMF levels. On the side of this meter there is a switch for normal and high settings. When the meter is set to high it will pick-up in the 1-5 milligauss range and on normal setting this will register 1-50 milligauss. Since we are normally looking for reading in the 1.5mg to 7 mg levels we would always use the high setting.

The cell sensor EMF detector requires a 9 volt battery and has a simple slide cover for access to the battery compartment.

KII EMF detectors have become very popular since seen on television. I have come to appreciate that this is a very sensitive meter and one I no longer use just for normal EMF detection. This is a single axis meter and is relatively inexpensive, below $100.00. The effective range of this meter is approximately12 feet.

Similar to most other meters, this will register ELF and VLF or Very Low Frequency EMF in Milligauss. It detects the ELF range (50 to 1,000Hz) & VLF range (1,000 to 20,000Hz). I have begun to utilize this meter as a communication device alone. I place it on a flat surface and demonstrate how to wave a hand in front it to make the lights go up and down which will register a fluctuation in the nearby electromagnetic field.

These devices come in several varieties now. When they first came out, you needed to keep a constant pressure on the switch, otherwise it would fluctuate; indicating a reading. This was almost impossible and that is why you may have seen several of the TV shows utilize coins on the face in order to keep the constant pressure on the switch. You can easily modify these devices yourself, but I suggest you order one that will have a built in switch, so that does not require constant pressure.

There are 5 lights on face of this meter dark green, light green, yellow, orange and red. When using this meter you need to remember what the lights mean, again we are looking for a measurement in the 1.5 to 7 mg range. The yellow light on this meter is what you want to see as the maximum light. Anything higher is a measurement of 10 mg and above.

The KII EMF detector requires a 9 volt battery. The battery compartment is on the back of the device and must be removed with a small screw driver to access the compartment.

ELF Zone EMF detector is the most economical device we will talk about, it can be purchased for under $20.00. The ELF name of the meter should indicate what it measures, Extremely Low Frequency EMF and it operates in the Frequency Bandwidth: ELF/VLF 20 - 10,000 Hz. The effective range of this meter is approximately10 feet.

There is a simple on/off switch on the right hand side of the meter and the face has 3 lights on it, green = 0 - 2.5 mg , yellow = 2.5 - 7 mg and red = 8 mg or higher . The range we are looking for is a fluctuation into the yellow light that is approximately within 2.5 to 7 mg.

The ELF Zone EMF detector requires a 9 volt battery. The battery compartment is on the back of the device and must be removed with a small screw driver to access the compartment.

Digital EMF detector is one instrument that I have used when I do a preliminary and/or base line readings at a location. The digital EMF meter is a single axis meter and registers frequency bandwidth: 30 to 300 Hz (ELF frequency range).It will give an accurate reading from 0.1 mg to 199.9 mg. The effective range of this meter is approximately 10 feet.

There is a simple on/off switch on the right hand side of the meter and an LED display face. This meter does have a propping device on the back of the meter which will allow it to stand up. You can easily read this meter with a flashlight.

The digital EMF detector requires a 9 volt battery. The battery compartment is on the back of the device.

Mel 8704 EMF detector will register ELF in a range down to 30Hz which is 20Hz lower than the KII EMF detector. This meter is one of the first built for the paranormal community and it has become one of my favorite meters in the case.

This meter has a front display backlit LED panel with an on/off switch on the front. Once the meter is turned on you will need to verify that it is set to Fahrenheit (F) or Celsius (C) whichever is your preference and then adjust the measurement value to milligauss. This meter also comes with a small tripod for upright mounting if you are going to place it in a constant position.

This meter also utilizes a small ambient probe on the end of the meter. I use this meter for a preliminary walk thru to do both temperature and EMF baselines prior to an investigation.

The Mel 8704 EMF detector requires a 9 volt battery. The battery compartment is on the back of the device and is accessed by a single screw.

Temperature recording devices:

Most of what you see today is known as non-contact IR thermometers. These devices will measure surface temperature of an object that is as far away as 100 feet (30 meters). These devices read the infrared energy naturally emitted from all objects. Basically this is thermal radiation. This may lead to a couple of questions:

What is Radiation?

Radiation is a method of heat transfer that does not rely upon any contact between the heat source and the heated object. For example, we feel heat from the sun even though we are not touching it. Heat can be transmitted though empty space by thermal radiation. Thermal radiation (often called infrared radiation) is a type of electromagnetic radiation (or light). Radiation is a form of energy transport consisting of electromagnetic waves traveling at the speed of light. No mass is exchanged and no medium is required.

Objects emit radiation when high energy electrons in a higher atomic level fall down to lower energy levels. The energy lost is emitted as light or electromagnetic radiation. Energy that is absorbed by an atom causes its electrons to "jump" up to higher energy levels. All objects absorb and emit radiation. When the absorption of energy balances the emission of energy, the temperature of an object stays constant. If the absorption of energy is greater than the emission of energy, the temperature of an object rises. If the absorption of energy is less than the emission of energy, the temperature of an object falls.

What is infrared?

Every form of matter with a temperature above absolute zero emits infrared radiation according to its temperature; this is known as characteristic radiation. The cause of this is the internal mechanical movement of molecules. The intensity of this movement depends on the temperature of the object. Since the molecule movement represents charge displacement, electromagnetic radiation (photon particles) is emitted.

These photons move at the speed of light and behave according to the known optical principles. They can be deflected, focused with a lens or reflected from reflective surfaces. The spectrum of this radiation ranges from 0.7 to 1000 um wavelength. For this reason, this radiation cannot be seen with the naked eye. This area lies within the red area of visible light and has therefore been called "infra"-red after the Latin.

IR thermometers can measure the surface temperature of an object as far as 100 feet (30 Meters) away. They do this utilizing an infrared sensor that travels out from the face of the device in a circular patter until it reaches a surface to measure. The problem I have seen is that the further away the object the larger the "circle" of coverage is. Therefore you cannot be certain of the exact area being measured. Realize when you use a laser pointed device the laser dot is the center of your circle, not the area being measured. It is best to use these devices indoors and at a maximum length of 25-30 feet for accuracy reasons only.

To use this device to obtain a room temperature you need to average out what you see on the device. Use a spray paint motion and start at an upper corner of a room and go to the opposite corner and continue to work your way down the wall. This will give you an average surface temperature of that wall which is nominally within 1 or 2 degrees of the ambient temperature of the space. Do this to all of the walls in the room.

At various points of your investigation you should "spot" check the location for any temperature variations. Use the spray paint motion in the room and if there are any entities in the space that pass thru the coverage area you may see a sudden drop or rise in the temperature. You would like to see a temperature difference of 5-10 degrees. If you do you may have something paranormal occurring.

These devices can also be fitted with an ambient probe. Ambient temperature is the temperature of the air in the room. This is what your wall thermostat measures at home. This is called a thermal couple device. A thermocouple or thermocouple thermometer is a junction between two different metals that produces a voltage related to a temperature difference. Thermocouples are a widely used type of temperature sensor for measurement and control and can also be used to convert heat into electric power. They are inexpensive and interchangeable, are supplied fitted with standard connectors, and can measure a wide range of temperatures.

Passive Infrared motion sensor:

A Passive Infrared motion sensor is a device that measures infrared (IR) light radiating from objects in its field of view. Motion is detected when an infrared source with one temperature, such as a human, passes in front of an infrared source with another temperature, such as a wall. All objects emit what is known as black body radiation. It is usually infrared radiation that is invisible to the human eye but can be detected by electronic devices designed for such a purpose. The term *passive* in this instance means that the device does not emit an infrared beam but merely passively accepts incoming infrared radiation.

These are inexpensive devices that can be purchased at any home center for under $30.00. These would typically be placed in a location where there is believed activity to occur. We have placed these devices on stairs and in doorways. Some devices are sensitive enough to pick up a mouse if it happen to pass in front of it, so be aware of that if you are in a location that these little critters may also be.

Typically there are 2 settings on these devices, chime and alarm. You can set this to your preference but from experience the chime is better. The alarm can rattle anyone in the area when it is triggered and you may need to go to the device to reset it each time it is triggered. When in the chime mode it sounds like the chime we all have heard when we enter a store. It will also only chime when there is an instance of temperature change. Once it is indicated it will reset itself.

That is all of the basic equipment you may want to purchase. Hopefully you have a better understanding now of what each piece does and why we use it.

7. Weather

You ask yourself why a paranormal investigative group is concerned with the weather. If you have an outdoor investigation you need to know how to dress. There are many other reasons why the weather is important to such groups; here are a few key points:

Humidity is a key factor due to excessive water vapor in the air which may give false positive photos. Relative humidity is a measurement of the amount of water vapor in the air compared to the maximum amount possible at a given temperature. Air with a relative humidity of 50% is holding half the total amount of water vapor it is capable of holding at that temperature.

Temperature and humidity combined are also necessary to know and understand. The "dew point" is the temperature at which air saturation occurs, and condensation begins. If air at 100% humidity is cooled, condensation will form as fog in the air or on surfaces at or below this dew point temperature (cold glass window of a heated house).This phenomenon may also be observed on a cold winter day when you "see your breath" in the air; your warm breath is cooled enough to condense part of its water vapor, producing the tiny water droplets as fog. This "fog" maybe viewed as a false positive photo.

It is said that with an incoming storm is you can smell the ozone in the air. Storms will produce an abundance of negatively charged ions in the air; this is similar to static electricity, which is excess energy in which spirits can tap into and manifest.

Excessive temperature, as well as extreme low temperature will adversely affect some of the meters used in paranormal research.

Rain, Snow and Fog will all produce false positive photos. Please refer to chapter 5 for some discussion on these items.

Lower temperatures are also good for investigating, why? Static electricity can build up much easier during the winter when the air is dryer. In the summer the humidity does not allow for static electricity to build. So in the colder months there is additional electrical energy in the air to help the spirits become more active.

The Sun and the Moon affect paranormal investigations also. It is a fact that solar flare activity will generate a large amount of excess energy in the atmosphere. This excess energy may be utilized by a spirit to manifest. With this overabundance of energy the amount of spirit activity seen is usually higher than normal.

The geomagnetic fields are strongest during the full and new moons. This also attributes to energy in which the spirit realm taps into and becomes more active.

Space Weather:

Solar flare: The Sun frequently emits plumes of energy, essentially bursts of solar wind. These solar flares contain gamma rays and X-rays, plus energized particles (protons and electrons). Energy can be equal to a billion megatons of TNT being released in a matter of minutes. Flare activity picks up as sunspots increase.

Solar flare classification:

Solar flares are classified based on their output of X-ray energy at the peak of their burst.

C-class flares are common
M-class flares are larger but moderately powerful
X-class flares are the most powerful

How does space weather affect what we are doing?

Solar X-rays: M CLASS FLARE
Geomagnetic Field: QUIET

Geomagnetic Storms: Also known as a magnetic storm is a disturbance of the Earth's upper atmosphere brought on by solar flares, bright eruptions from the visible portion of the Sun's chromosphere. The material associated with these flares consists primarily of protons and electrons with the energy of a few thousand electron volts. called plasma. This material moves through the interplanetary medium at speeds ranging from 1,000 to 2,000 km (600 to 1,200 miles) per second, so that the ejected material reaches the Earth in approximately 21 hours. The pressure of the incoming plasma is transmitted to the outer edge of the Earth's magnetosphere; this causes an increase in the observed geomagnetic field at the ground, perhaps through hydromagnetic waves. One of the results of such activity is the visible aurora (Northern and lights) and the aurora australis which is the similar lights at the South Pole.

For the paranormal investigator this simply means there is more energy around for spirits to tap into.

The Moon: Lunar Phases affect the earth's geomagnetic fields. As most police officers and emergency room doctors will tell you, when the moon is full they are quite busy. A full moon exhibits more energy onto the earth which in turn allows for the possibility of an increase in paranormal activity. By keeping track of the lunar cycle we may be able to pinpoint when paranormal activity is at its height as it relates to all weather, sun and moon phenomenon.

8. Forming Your Team

One aspect of paranormal investigation that doesn't receive any press or any hype is the investigation team itself. Some groups may only have a small amount of members so the team is basically established from the beginning. Other groups are larger and need to be somewhat selective when it comes to placing a team into a location. You cannot just send the entire group out to a location that should only have 4 team members.

The manner in which a team is selected for any given investigation varies from group to group. This is in no way meant to say this is the only way to accomplish this task, it is just saying this is a way to do so. The first chapter of this book we mentioned that you need to be honest with yourself which comes into play here. If you have effectively communicated your short comings then the person putting together the team will understand what you and the team requirements are to be successful.

When we receive a case, we like to understand the location and the client a little bit prior to going out for the investigation. We like to set-up a time where we will go to the location and discuss the case and the clients concerns with them face to face. This helps us with a few factors for establishing the proper team to attend. We see the location and now can determine the correct amount of investigators needed to properly cover the location without tripping over each other. It also gives us a better indication as to what is occurring and how to handle the client.

These are critical pieces to know. You never want to overload a location; this will only cause problems within your group's ability to collect viable evidence. It will also give you a better idea as to what you may encounter, the old cliché," you don't bring a knife to a gun fight" comes to mind. The clients concern and what they need is paramount, you may need to bring along one of your investigators that is capable of relaxing and calming the client. You may need a diverse group of intuitive investigators or psychics along with technical investigators. Experience is also important to the final selection of a team member. If it is a critical case where you are down to 2 people to select, you certainly wouldn't select a newbie over the seasoned veteran that has the field experience.

Too many people involved in groups take it as a personal attack when they are not selected for an investigation. Everyone needs to understand it is not a favoritism game. It is solely based on client and location needs. Everyone needs experience and when you are in a public location that is where you can start to hone your investigative skills before going into a private home.

Prior to investigation:

A team leader or TL should be selected and they should always:

- Find a meeting spot convenient to either the location or central to all of the investigators.
- Determine the time to meet properly allowing enough time for travel.
- Send an email out or call the team telling them this information at least 2 days prior, do not list the smaller teams in this email. In other words don't say Tom and Esther are teamed together, wait until you are on site for that. What if Tom backs out or if he and Esther really dislike each other? You don't want to foster any feelings leading into an investigation.
- Review the questionnaire so you understand what the main purpose for being there is. Do not share this with the team so they will not be predisposed to something. In chapter 13 we will discuss the questionnaire in more detail.
- On the day of the investigation you should have the weather information and the moon/solar information written down a placed into the case file.

9. What to Expect on an Investigation

For those that are starting out in this field there is a lot you will need to learn and understand before you actually go out and do a case. One thing I think all of the "newbie's" out there need to understand is; "Do not expect anything to happen."

If you go on an investigation expecting to see the ghost of George Washington or just Aunt Emma, you are setting yourself up to be disappointed. Most of the time paranormal investigators are sitting around waiting and waiting and waiting. Paranormal activity doesn't begin just because an investigator is present. If you go in expecting nothing to be there and for nothing to be paranormal, then you won't be disappointed.

If you are at a private home of a client and you are there to help them, keep control of your emotions. You never want to seem excited or disappointed in front of them. They are looking to you for help, so your body language and attitude is easily picked up by them. You need to be as even tempered as you possibly can thru an investigation. This holds true for the time when something does happen as well. Don't run out of the house when Aunt Emma is speaking to you; remember the famous "Dude Run" from one of those television shows. If you are helping someone then you need to act accordingly.

I have been on several investigations when something amazing has happened. I am also happy to say that when it did, we went about our business as usual. When we got into the car for the ride home, that's when we said to each other, "Did you see that?" In front of the client we remained professional. As always remember that you are representing more than yourself while doing this, you are representing the paranormal community.

While not expecting anything to occur; you should be prepared when something does. If you see an apparition in the room with you and all you do is look at it then you have nothing to prove what has happened. Have your camera at hand to snap several photographs of the area, have an IR thermometer to scan the area for any temperature fluctuations. Hopefully you are in a position to conduct an EVP session and you have your EMF meters to see if they can registered anything.

Types of hauntings/ghosts:

The general Hollywood concept of a ghost is not accurate but it's what many think about when they speak of ghosts. There are basically three types of hauntings.

The first type of haunting is exactly like a video playback of a historic or tragic event. This is known as a residual haunting. The event unfolds in front of you and there is no interaction between you and the ghosts. They seem to not notice you and go through the motions of the event that occurred in the past. This event has been imprinted on the area or building and is replayed back later when conditions are right. The ghosts that you see in this type are not earthbound spirits; they are just visual play backs. Since everything is made up of energy, the theory is that some of the energy from an event can be recorded by certain materials and played back when the atmosphere triggers it. Remember that video and audio tape is just oxidized (rust) film that enables the images and sounds to "stick" to it. This type may be frightening when you see it, but you are in no danger so enjoy the experience.

The second type of haunting is an interactive spirit that manifests in many ways. You may see a full bodied or partial bodied apparition. More frequently than that, you may hear voices, music, footsteps, etc. You may also smell odors which sources cannot be found (i.e. pipe tobacco when no one smokes). You may also see orbs, mists, and other light effects. You may feel touches, cold spots, and other light physical contact. This ghost is the spirit of a deceased human being. They may be stuck here (earthbound) for reasons such as tragic sudden death, fear of moving on, guilt, or unfinished business. They also could be here visiting loved ones or to warn or pass along a message. These human spirits are the same as they were in life, so they may be good or bad, but not really evil. Think of all the people you know, probably a bit of good and bad, some worse than others.

This type can cause some scary situations but you must think about the situation they are in, you don't see them but they see you. They will try to get your attention any way they can. Many times this is the terrifying event that people will write to me about like the lights going on and off, items moving, noises, etc. For the most part these are just attention getters and nothing more.

There are a few more mischievous human spirits that will do these things to bother you and scare you on purpose. They may just be a prankster or maybe they want you to leave the old home or not to change something in the home. They have all the same motivations you and I would have. These human spirits account for a majority of the hauntings we encounter and are relatively harmless. Yes, there are extreme cases and sometimes they can cause dangerous situations, but this is not the norm.

The third type of ghost you may encounter is not a rare one, but is rare that they interact with the living. They are non human spirits, commonly known as demons and devils. They are mentioned in the bible numerous places in both the old and new testaments. People like Ed and Lorraine Warren have been dealing with this type of spirit for years. This type is dangerous and can cause you harm.

I believe that if there is good, there must be a counter balance, evil. These non human spirits often disguise themselves as friendly and helpful human spirits. They often appear in cases dealing with Ouija boards, black magic and satanic worship. This is why I recommend not trying to contact spirits and doing ghost hunts without some understanding of what's out there. It's also why I recommend you go with or learn from experienced people before hand. That way you can ghost hunt with relative safety from these entities.

Types of Spirits:

Apparitions: better known as ghosts appear to be some form of the human mind (consciousness, personality, soul, and/or spirit) that functions apart from the body and may survive the death of the body. They have the personality and emotions and act and dress like the person they were when alive. Reports of apparitions fall into four broad categories.

Apparitions from another Dimension or Time: There are reports of apparitions who act as frightened of us as we are of them. It is believed that these apparitions indicate that we, not they are the ghosts. In reports such as these the observed "ghosts" appear to be alive.

Apparitions of the Dead: These are apparitions of people who have generally been dead longer than 12-48 hours. There are two subsets:
   1. those that make one or several visits to someone (they may not have known this person while alive)

2. The very rare cases of apparitions that linger for months or years around a particular location or person that they associated with when alive.

Apparitions of the Living: Also called bilocation, apparitions can be either spontaneous or intentional. In the case of spontaneous bilocation, the person whose apparition is seen is generally (though not always) unaware of his/her bilocation.

Bilocation is considered intentional when the apparition can be connected to a person who was aware s/he was having an out of body experience (OBE), or with someone who was consciously trying to communicate with the person who witnessed his/her apparition.

Crisis Apparitions: Apparitions of the dying or recently dead (usually less than twelve hours, but as much as 24-48 hours) are the most frequently reported of apparitions. This category commonly involves one-time visits to someone with whom the apparition has close emotional ties. Though the encounter usually seems to be a type of farewell, sometimes important and useful information is relayed to the viewer.

Poltergeists: This phenomenon typically involves a connection to a living individual at the location. There are mostly associated with pre-teen female dealing with unresolved emotional or stress issues. They will use psychokinesis to create a physical disturbance or possibly even a manifestation. The agent involved with this activity typically does not realize they are the underlying cause. One of the most documented physical items with poltergeist activity is the stacking of various objects.

Sensitivity to Spirits:

Is it possible for something more to occur while on an investigation? That is something that cannot be calculated or approximated. One thing we do know is that people that are open or sensitive to spirits can pick-up on quite a few things while on an investigation.

Everyone is born with some level of sensitivity. As we grow we are trained to turn off this ability and therefore it remains dormant. As children we are more open and that may be why several children have "imaginary friends". Almost everyone can remember a childhood dream of someone in the closet or under the bed that was quickly dispelled by mom or dad by simply saying," There is nothing there."

This is how we are trained to turn off this ability. However it can be re-energized or re-stimulated. Many paranormal investigators do claim they can now "feel" things that they could not before. More than likely it is simply a fact that they did not understand what they were feeling in the first place but now they can make the proper association.

There several different aspects of sensitivity to spirits and they have commonly been referred to as the "Clair" sisters, and they are:

Clairaudience – Is a form of channeling. Usually defined as, the perception of messages in thought forms from an entity that exists in another realm. The person receiving these messages "hears" the messages in their mind. Though words or songs may actually be heard the same way one "hears" a phrase or song running through their heads, the thought itself may be all that's transmitted. For the budding clairaudient: Be sure you share the messages obtained through clairaudience only with people who understand. Clairaudience has often been confused with schizophrenia.

Clairgustance - is being aware of tastes without actually placing anything into the mouth. These sensitives are able to perceive the essence of a substance through taste from the spiritual realms.

Clairsentience - Also known as Psychometry, and is the ability to touch or hold onto an object, stand in a specific place, or touch the body of a person and sense the energy encircling that person, place or thing. Energies can be light or heavy, joyful or foreboding, tough or gentle, peaceful or angry, good or evil, and are judged by the emotional impact on the clairsentient. A clairsentient is an empathic person who is able to experience and translate all kinds of energies.

Clairvoyance - Clairvoyance is the art of 'seeing' with senses beyond the five we normally use. Clairvoyance is often called the 'sixth sense'. A clairvoyant see's with what is commonly referred to as the third eye. In the human body there is a gland called the pineal gland. This gland has degenerated from its original size comparable to a ping pong ball to its present size comparable to a pea, because we forgot how to use it a long time ago.

The pineal gland looks like an eye, and in some respects, it is literally an eyeball. It is round and has an opening on one portion. In that opening is a lens for focusing light. It looks upward. It's hollow and it has color receptors inside. Some people become clairvoyant after a unique experience such as a Near Death Experience, high fever, serious accident, blow to the head area, etc. Clairvoyance connects to the right side of the brain - the feminine, creative, and intuitive aspects.

That is why you may tend to feel physical sensations on the left side of your body when you work clairvoyantly. The energy enters in through the left side of your body so as to activate the right side of your brain. Young children and teenagers still remember that there is a special connection between realities - but adults - unless having accessed these gifts in childhood - generally forget and move into 3D stuff to fill up their time. They leave the higher frequency work to their higher consciousness in dreamtime. They call / rely upon that connection only in times of emergency or when they ask for guidance from a higher aspect of themselves.

10. Conducting an Investigation

This sounds pretty simple doesn't it? Go out and have at it right? I wish it were only that easy. As with anything good, you need to understand a few things before you wander into the local hot spot.

First what the difference is between a ghost hunt and a paranormal investigation. A ghost hunt is where you go out to a location and you literally hunt to see what you can find. You act as if it is a normal investigation but you don't know if there are any spirits roaming around the place. An investigation is where you are going into a known haunted location. That being said whenever you go out to a client's home for the first visit you are more than likely doing a ghost hunt.

Before you leave for an investigation:

Let's quickly discuss the importance of you on an investigation. You are the most important tool that will be utilized at the investigation, make sure you are clear headed, sharp and prepared to stay focused. You may be entering a night where all you will do is talk in the dark for the next several hours or you could have the investigation you always hoped for. The point is not to expect anything and be as level headed as you can before you go out.

I happened to be watching one of the paranormal TV shows recently, the one where they say they are completely scientific and that is the best way for them to investigate. They had a "guest" investigator that said when they entered a certain room they had a bad feeling. So the scientific investigators asked, "Did the hair on your neck stand up?" The guest replied that it had. That's when the scientific investigators said, "You know that is your body's natural defense mechanism warning you that something is in there."

So these proponents of strictly scientific approaches recognize the importance of what you, the investigators are feeling during the investigation. These are the types of psychic impressions which I have spoken of throughout this book. I said this just to show you that even those that denounce the "touchy feely" side of investigating believe in some version of it.

If you are going out to an investigation after a bad day at the office and the traffic today is entirely too much to handle at the moment making you angry, than tonight may not be the best night for you to go out and participate in an investigation. Simply put, like attracts like. If you are in a nasty state of mind, you may very well attract something nasty and there is no need to put your team, client and yourself into that situation.

To investigate properly you need to be in the right state of mind. Calm and relaxed and prepared for what may come your way. Common sense dictates that you should never drink alcohol or use any form of illegal substances at least 24 hours prior to an investigation. This way you know you will be clear headed when you begin.

Now that we are actually starting to investigate it is important to talk about being skeptical. Most people say that if you are a skeptic you cannot join in on a paranormal investigation. I believe there is some leeway here that needs to be mentioned. I believe that all investigators need to be an open minded skeptic. Not completely turned against everything but also not believing everything out there is paranormal. This means that you are willing to take into consideration the possibility of something paranormal existing after the natural has been eliminated from the equation.

The opposite holds true too, you cannot go out on an investigation believing everything you will come across is paranormal. You need to always have a level head and be looking for natural explanations first. Once the natural has been removed then the paranormal will come into play.

How to dress for an investigation:

You need to dress comfortably and safely for the environment in which you will be investigating. Many people I know like to wear clothing with many pockets. You will quickly see the wisdom behind this decision.

Shoes are very important. Make sure they are comfortable and preferably silent; you don't want something like cowboy boots on a hard wood floor. You should not wear any jewelry or reflective clothing. Basic colors work the best they do not look brighter or duller in the light used on an investigation.

For those with long hair, this should be neatly tied back to prevent your hair from going in front of your camera lens during the investigation.

Do not wear any fragrances, your sense of smell is very important. We have all heard of smelling flowers when some spirits are around so we do not want to confuse another investigator with a fragrance you are wearing.

Try to look as professional as possible, this doesn't mean shirt and ties but it does mean you should look respectable. Do not wear any provocative clothing, yes girls this can be a distraction even in the dark. I know of too many instance where, oops never mind I can't say that here. You and your group need to be represented in a positive light; the paranormal field is already looked upon with questions, so do all you can here to bring a better light to it.

On site arrival:

We are going on the assumption that you already have permission to be on the site where the investigation is going to take place. If not stop and leave now, you must always have permission to be in any location. We have a release form that we ask our clients to sign indicating they have given us access to the location to conduct a paranormal investigation. We have releases also for them that say we will not hold them liable for any personal injury we may receive by conducting this investigation. Some people are always afraid of being sued and this helps alleviate that for them.

Earlier we spoke about a leader for an investigation; this is the person that is in charge on that particular investigation. You should never have more than one person in charge on an investigation; it will just complicate what you are trying to do.

The team leaders (TL) will set-up a meeting location and time so you can show up at a location as inconspicuous as possible. Your clients are already concerned over what is happening to them and you certainly do not want to bring attention to your arrival. Once you arrive at the location the TL should introduce the team members to the client and also remind the client not to speak to anyone about the case. You do not want any team members predisposed to the activity reported.

The TL should know this information and therefore any question need to be directed to them.

Once you have set your equipment in a convenient location the TL should ask to take the team around the location. While doing so the TL should have someone take initial or base line readings in each room during this walk through.

The base line readings will give you something to measure against for all electromagnetic field detectors and temperature devices. To do these you will need a digital EM detector and a thermometer. Inside of each room you need to walk around and measure floor to ceiling every 2-3 square feet of floor space. You will take a large amount of reading in each room. Once the room is completed you than need to average out these readings and establish your baseline. This seems like it will take some time, and it may, but it is extremely important to your investigation.

During the walk thru the TL should reiterate the room names to be utilized so every team member hears them and understands which room is what. By doing this the team has an understanding of the layout and associated room names.

While doing the walk through take notes on reflective surfaces, you will see them. The TL should ask about closing drapes and shades to help eliminate any outside contamination. If you are investigating in the summer and these windows are your ventilation just take notes on what could affect your investigation.

Establishing the teams:

After the initial walk through the TL now needs to be assign team members to each other, typically you would like to place a more experienced investigator with a less experienced one. This way there is always some learning going on for the newer team members. I have always waited to assign team members until we have arrived on site in case someone had to cancel out or an unexpected argument between members that day, you just never know. Teams should be a minimum of two (2) people. I have seen the TV shows where they send people off to do solo vigils, but I believe these are a bad thing to do. What if something happens to that individual there is no one there to help them. If the activity happens to be intense, there are more eyes and ears there to document what is going on. In the scenario above if the activity is too much for someone to handle, they have a much better chance of staying through it if they have someone with them.

With a minimum of two (2) members to each team you can now split and check the equipment. You want to make sure that you use as much equipment as possible and that it is evenly distributed from team to team. Each member should each have their own camera, digital voice recorder or a pad and paper and a flash light. Hopefully there is an equipment bag where they could take a couple of EMF detectors, an IR thermometer and if possible a motion sensor. Hopefully there is enough equipment available to accomplish that.

At this point there should be a final check of all batteries and times on all devices; voice recorders, watches and cameras and you want to have all times within a minute of each other for when you are reporting your investigation.

The rotation:

You now have paired teams with appropriate equipment, I have always asked that if you took a piece of equipment from one of the cases you are the one that would return it to that case and carry it with you for the entire investigation. The TL would now assign the teams to different areas at the location, for this let's assume we are in a 2 story private home with a full basement and we have 4 investigators present. You would like to keep a floor open between each team if possible and rotate the teams through each floor as the investigation continues. We normally would investigate from 9 pm to 12 am and this would allow for 3 one hour rotations through the location.

With this set-up I would start one team in the basement and one team on the second floor leaving the first floor open, at the first rotation I would have the teams move to the next area by having the second floor team head into the basement and the basement team to the first floor. After an hour the first floor team to the second floor and finally the basement team to the first floor. These last 2 rotations there needs to be communication between the teams to minimize possible contamination with EVP work etc.

How to investigate:

Once you know the location that you will begin in, get to that location as quickly and quietly as you can. Once there quickly survey the room and make a determination of where you will set-up your equipment and start placing it. As you position each piece make a note of it on your recorder or pad of paper for your reference. Note which EMF meter by name is where and the area that it is covering.

In a small house you want to find a spot to sit down and try to keep movement to a minimum. If you have an hour on the second floor and there are 4 bedrooms try to spend at least 15 minutes in each bedroom. When you start, make a note of the room you are in and the time.

Also make note of any reflective surfaces, i.e. mirrors or glass front cabinets and televisions to name a few. If there are any reflective metal components to the furniture in the room try to note it. Make note of outside light sources that could affect your photos, street lights, traffic etc.

You need to work as a team, always stay within view of each other if possible, if not stay within ear shot so you can effectively communicate and help each other if necessary. Never assume you are close enough to your partner, make sure you are.

After a period of time you will move to another room or location. Make a note of the time you move and where you go to. You may freely move about but realize in some locations your movement may sound like a response to a group of investigators elsewhere in the location. By recording your movement and time it can be determined if your movement and the other group's possible response could be one in the same thereby negating this episode as evidence. If there is any possibility that this was what the others heard it cannot be used as evidence because now there is possible contamination.

The main thing you will do while on an investigation is document everything you are doing and I mean everything. A slight cough or sneeze you do could sound like something completely different to the team downstairs and therefore should be noted by you as the one making the noise and by them as the ones hearing this noise.

Things you may not consider worth documenting but you should are:
- Coughing
- Sneezing
- Laughing
- Banging into an object
- Dropping anything
- Using the facilities when not on break
- Turning anything on that may generate an electrical flow in the location or noise, i.e. a TV.
- When doing a knocking experiment
- Slipping
- Gasping out loud

Hopefully you get the point now, **<u>DOCUMENT EVERYTHING</u>**.

Equipment placement:

You should have a variety of equipment with you and you are now ready to place it around the room you are in. A few chapters back we discussed the effective range of some of the more popular EMF detectors. Survey the room quickly and decide where to place each meter to properly cover the entire room. Refer to any notes you may have from the TL as to possible EMF contamination and avoid placing your meters in those areas. If you find a location that was overlooked by the TL let the team know at the next rotation, we all can save time when we communicate properly. Placing meters back to back is acceptable to get complete coverage of the room. You may not be able to achieve complete coverage but try to get as much of the space covered as you possibly can, that is your primary goal.

Now that you have made your preliminary notes and have placed your equipment try to settle down and let the space become accustomed to you. After a few minutes you may want to begin an EVP session, once again refer to that chapter for some techniques but remember if you are going to do an EVP session you need to make sure that you let your partner know so they can join in on the recording increasing your chances of getting an EVP, but also to let them know what you are doing to prevent any possible contamination. As you begin this remember to mention the time and location (which room) you are in for your report.

80

Be timely and pertinent with your line of questions and remember to try and keep the amount of recording time to a manageable level. If you are in a little girl's bedroom maybe you can ask some questions about the little girl or if the spirit was a parent, you will soon develop a method that works for you, just allow the feeling and emotion of the space work with you.

After a few minutes you may want to try another form of contact that is ok if you use some control. That is provoking. Now there are people that say you should never do this yet they are willing to only do EVP's which is also open to whomever. If you provide some control you may get a response that is acceptable.

This basically mean do not ask for something open ended. The worst question is: Can you give me a sign of your presence? This is open to interpretation by whatever is there with you and if they decide the sign should be a water pitcher being dumped over your head, that's great evidence but not quite what you wanted. Instead to ask them to replicate a knocking sound that you do or gently open the door to the room only while you are there. You need to make that clear, only do these things when you are there, you do not want to have a client calling you at 5 am saying the spirits are now opening and closing that bedroom door scaring all of them. Be clear that whatever you ask to happen only occurs when you are there.

Of course you have been making notes of everything that you asked for and whether or not you received a response. Now you take what we discussed here from room to room, always making notes for when you have changed locations and completed the investigation.

If you are frightened during your investigation, let your partner know and calmly walk out of the area. If you need to, exit the location completely letting the TL know what has happened. Do not run out and never just leave without saying something to another team member.

At the conclusion of the investigation I cannot tell you how many times I was asked by the client "what did you find?" This can be handled in 2 different ways. The first response should always be you don't know, because you don't really know yet. All you have to go on is your personnel experiences and they are not something you can base your investigation on. Tell them you need to review the evidence.

The exception I have used is if a client is in distress and needs some comforting and we definitely saw grandma there, I will them let them know that to help comfort them.

11. Client Relations

This is the part of the field that gets the least amount of publicity but is the driving force behind many groups out there. The reason we do what we do is to help people in their situations learn how to deal with what is happening. Yes I said deal with it. The reason I say this is because my personal belief is that as in life we have free will, once we make the transition I do not believe that is lost. So if we have free will when we transition and I choose to stay where I am at then who can "remove" me or make me "go into the light"?

Now this discussion is for human entities and will not discuss any inhuman activity. If that is occurring then get a team capable of handling that situation involved.

First Contact:

Typically a client will contact you either via email or phone, in either case it has taken something to have occurred for them to reach out. People shy away from the paranormal unless they are involved in either a haunting or research group, so imagine how this person must be feeling to go against what they believe to not exist and reach out to you. They may feel foolish or, as I have heard many times, "you'll think I'm crazy but". This is where your compassion needs to start with them immediately.

This client has reached out to you, and you need to respond to them within a timely manner. I like to get back to a client within 24 hours of the first contact. Your first response to them needs to be one of understanding and one that, if needed, will calm the client down. If you have a client screaming someone is trying to do them harm, you need to listen to them and start compiling data on what is happening. Most of the time, you will start to see a pattern develop and this will help you in working with them.

What I have noticed is that the client didn't see, hear or understand the earlier incidents as something paranormal. I usually try to talk to them to see what and when this actually started to happen. It is always the "big thing" that they notice. During our conversations they start to talk about "smaller" less scary things that have happened and I point that out to them.

They begin to see that whoever is there has been trying to reach out to them for some time and have slowly been escalating their attempts until that big moment when they finally got noticed.

I liken this to a child trying to get your attention. They will start with the small tug and say dad, dad, over and over until they just scream out DAD!! It escalates until you recognize them. Similar experiences have been reported to spirits hanging around; they have escalated what they were doing until they have gotten you attention.

Discus with the client what they are going through and be sure to listen carefully. Don't throw in your experience or feelings on their case up front. This is their time to tell you what is going on so be sure to listen carefully. The point to this is that after the initial contact you strive to have the client calmed down and assured you will be there for them during this process.

Restate what they have told you to be sure you understand their situation. Also you must reassure the client that they are not crazy if what they are experiencing is truly a paranormal event. If they are experiencing something other than a paranormal event you need to tell them you do not think this is a paranormal event and you cannot help them. I typically do not attempt a resolution at this point, but each case is different. You need to understand when someone is just asking a question or is in need of further assistance. If they need you to continue I send out a questionnaire. In Chapter 13 we will discuss a potential client questionnaire which will also help you in your final approach to helping this client.

Immediate help:

There are always cases which need to move to the front of the line. Typically these are the cases that involve children or inhuman activity. If a child is involved I typically schedule an immediate visit if possible. This is where you will need to educate the client so they can educate and properly calm the child.

This can be a difficult situation to be in so tread carefully. You will need to discuss what is going on with the child if you can, always be sure to do this with the parent in the room with you. During this interview listen carefully to the child but also pay attention to see if the parent is giving the answers to the child. This happens frequently so you will need to separate the facts from each story very carefully. This is an area of what we do where someone with clinical psychology is invaluable.

I have been blessed to have friends that can help me in these situations and I have always brought them along for that very reason. They can handle a child and I would address the problems with the parent. I cannot stress enough that this is a delicate process and needs to have the proper attention to correctly navigate through it.

Next Step:

After you have established an investigation is warranted the client may need someone to sit with them during the investigation. This person would need to be well versed in the process your team employs and also be able to comfort the client through the investigation. This is more common than you might realize, so remember to increase your team size by one person to be able to do this. Never discuss on site anything about the case with a client unless it is absolutely necessary. You really need to go back and evaluate your findings to properly answer any of their questions.

Just prior to leaving a clients home or business someone involved with the case should be introduced as the "follow-up" person to the client. This is a person that they now have met face to face and can identify with. If the client requested someone to be with them during the investigation I would ask that person to do the follow-up for the case. Also this is where you need to tell the client a time frame in which you will be through your review process and when they can expect to hear back from you on a final conclusion with your results,

After the investigation is a key spot to keep contact with the client. Many groups go in to do an investigation and never get back to a client. You must keep them updated on what is happening with their case.

Case manager/Follow-up person:

The majority of your clients will contact you either through email or a phone call. Once this contact is received the information will be forwarded to the case manager. The case manager should call the contact within 24-48 hours from the date that the client originally contacted you. This is done so they can introduce themselves to the client and to let them know that they will be answering any questions they might have prior to an investigation. The case manager will follow the client through the whole process of questionnaire, preliminary investigation, investigation and formal report.

The case manager will work with the group leaders and the client to establish a preliminary investigation date. This will be a date and time convenient to all involved. This will also allow the client and the case manager to meet face to face. This will help develop a trust with the case manager and the client.

Critical contact times for the case manager and client will be:
- Immediately after initial contact.
- After the investigation the case manager should call the client 1-2 days after.
  - Asking if there is any increase or decrease in activity
  - If so what was the activity
  - Has anyone in the home felt differently in anyway
  - Calm and reassure the client as necessary
  - Reiterate that the team members are doing their review.
  - Let the client know that you will be calling in another week to check on them. In the meantime if they have any questions or concerns let them contact you
- Follow up should be on a weekly basis until the client has the formal report.
- If you are asking for a second investigation the case manager should schedule that investigation.
- If there is a need for a second investigation follow up should continue on a bi weekly basis just to check on the state of the client.
- Case manager should confirm the date and time prior to the investigation date

After the second investigation the same process should be repeated. If there is no additional investigations to be scheduled and there was activity in the home there should be periodic phone calls made to the client just to keep lines of communication open to see if there is any additional activity at a later date.

If there is no activity found in the home and the client receives the report in the mail the case manager should call to make sure the client understands everything. If the case manager feels it necessary to make an additional phone call after that to check on the client they should do so.

Public Relations

Public relations (PR): is the practice of managing the flow of information between an organization and the general public. Public relations gain an organization or individual exposure to their audiences using topics of public interest and news items that do not require direct payment. Because public relations place exposure in credible third-party outlets, it offers a third-party legitimacy that advertising does not have. Common activities include speaking at conferences and working with the press.

Public relations can be used to build rapport with clients, libraries, or the general public. Almost any organization that has a stake in how it is portrayed in the public arena employs some level of public relations.

A public relations person is basically an image shaper. Their job is to generate positive publicity for your group and enhance your reputation to the general public. The public relations person must be a good communicator in print, in person and on the phone.

They must be able to cultivate and maintain contacts with journalists, set up speaking engagements, respond to inquiries and speak directly to the press on behalf of your group. They must keep lines of communication open.

In this position you will be required to know:
- The history of your group and how much experience it has.
- Your groups standards and protocols for investigations
- Equipment used by your group
- Reporting time frames for a client to expect an answer or reports if you are going to do them.

12. Reporting Your Evidence

How evidence is reported varies from team to team and can consist of an online reporting system such as ParaDB or be done in a simple word document. The important thing to remember is that this is where you need to indicate what you did and what your conclusion is to the client. This is your product to your client. This is how you will be viewed by the client and possibly in the paranormal community. So you want to be as clear and consistent as possible at this stage.

Professionalism is the goal here, the more organized and structured you come across to a client the better they will feel with your involvement. Offer your opinion on the case and suggest possible resolutions to them. Just telling them something is active and leaving them out there alone is not very professional.

It is import that each investigator that involved provides a report that will explain what they did and what time this occurred. Never discuss what another investigator did or said unless you have evidence supporting them. I have seen many reports over the years and I am a believer in an accurate timeline style of reporting by each investigator.

An important tool every investigator should have is a pen and paper or a voice recorder. Whenever you do anything write it down with a time reference or record it. This is the basic start of your timeline.

A report should always include the following:
1. Investigators name
2. Location of the investigation
   - Client names and address
3. Date of the investigation
4. Time of the investigation from start to finish
5. The equipment being used
   - Electro Magnetic Field (EMF) detectors by style/name
     - ELF Zone EMF detector
     - Cell Sensor EMF detector
     - etc

   List Voice recorders by manufacturer i.e. Sony
   - Were any data loggers used?
   - Were any motion detectors used?
6. What was done
7. Impressions? See below for more description.
8. A conclusion

I believe some further elaboration is required here. Items numbered 1 through 5 are pretty self explanatory so let's take this one step at a time and start with number 6.

What was done – This is the meat of a report, it is important to explain what was done from your point of view. As I have said I believe in an accurate timeline to report what was done. To do this just remember when, where and what times 2 (maybe more)

- **When** – hopefully you understand that this is the time of day i.e. 9:30 pm.
- **Where** – which room were you in. Dining room.
- **What times 2** – What were you using (equipment)
- **what happened?** All together this would look like this:

9:30 pm – We relocated into the dining room and I used my digital voice recorder in an attempt to record an EVP. I recorded the following EVP which is saying "Hello there", ms1mpd930pm.wav – This time line contains the when 9:30 pm, the where - dining room, the first what - digital voice recorder, followed by the second what – an attempt to record an EVP.

You should always synchronize your digital voice recorder, cameras and watches prior to the stat of an investigation. This way all team members are coordinated. You need to be sure you list everything within your timeline. If you sneeze on the second floor that may have sound like an anomalous event to a team on the first floor so list it. When the team leader is reviewing everything they will need to pick out that one cancels out the other. Don't forget to list what time you changed rooms, your walking could sound like a response asked for by another team member somewhere else in the home or building.

Always list what equipment was placed where and what area it was covering. This helps in your tallies and helps you determine what pieces of equipment are giving you the best results or which pieces are ready to be replaced.

When you investigate you will be using a large variety of equipment. For example you may enter a room with 2 ELF zone EMF detectors, 1 cell sensor EMF detector, 2 KII EMF detectors not mention your voice recorder and digital camera. Well when you indicate a positive reading on an EMF detector which one was it and what area was it covering? Without listing all of the pertinent information you are losing a valuable tool in your research.

An example of this utilizing the list above I would start a new timeline once the equipment is placed and I would note it as follows:

9:03 pm – I placed an ELF zone EMF detector on the center coffee table covering the area in front of the front window. I placed the second ELF zone EMF detector on the opposite end of the coffee table covering the entrance to the dining room. I placed the cell sensor EMF detector on the table adjacent to the entrance hall covering the entrance into the living room. I placed one KII EMF detector on the fire place mantle covering the center of the room. I placed the final KII EMF detector on the sofa next to where I was sitting.

That's a lot of information in that timeline entry but it covers everything you carried into the room and where it is placed. Why do you want to do this? A simple explanation is that the room is completely covered; the rest of this explanation is that you can see if there is any movement through the room and where it started from and ended. It is beneficial in another way as well. If the team on the floor is directly above or below and they are starting to experience something or ask for a response, you could see that response in your meters. This is where the timeline/location comes into play. If you did not use this technique you could miss that the one team was asking for something and you were recording the result of that. Because of the timeline you can correlate that anomalous event.

What should you not concern yourself with recording? Well that is a slightly loaded question because you want to record everything. An example of what I did not typically record would be "random" photographs. Whenever I walked into a room I would take several photos around that room prior to beginning my investigation. Also during an investigation I would just randomly snap a photo here or there. If I caught an anomaly in one of these photographs it was always easy enough to look at the photo data to get a time and I would add into my time line.

OK we have now ended the investigation and we need to review and look over all of our evidence. Do we label evidence in any way? One word, absolutely. If we do not properly label the evidence how can we correlate it to anything? Remember we are presenting a product to a client and we need to be clear and consistent.

I learned a way to name evidence from a group I once belonged to and I still believe it is a great way to name/label evidence. The name of this EVP mentioned above is ms1mpd930pm.wav. There is a lot of information within this name and it ties the evidence into the report by naming it this way. Let's break it down to explain it for you.

The name contains the following information in it which keeps this particular piece of evidence associated with the correct case at all times and this is how: (location name) ms – (trip number) 1 – (investigator) mpd – (time) 930pm .wav or .jpg (audio or photo file) You can also utilize this for video clips. Whenever you look at the evidence name you immediately know the case and the person that captured the evidence. This also ties neatly into you timeline for easy reference.

With the advent of various cameras and different meters we have every investigator log indicate the following. This allows us to keep track of what equipment is providing the most successful pieces of evidence.

This is an example of an individual investigation report. Note the wording and how everything is explained out.

Name:

Date of Investigation:

Location:

Time:

Equipment Used: (list any personal equipment of yours)

Physical evidence:

With the advent of various cameras and different meters we have every investigator log indicate the following. This allows us to keep track of what equipment is providing the most successful pieces of evidence.

Photos:
Total number of digital photos: 52
Total number of positive digital photos: 2

Total number of IR digital photos: 25
Total number of positive IR digital photos: 1
Total number of Full spectrum digital photos: 20
Total number of positive Full spectrum digital photos: 1
Locations of all Positive Photos: i.e. living room (2) -
ms1mpd930pm.jpeg, ms1mpd931pm.jpeg, Bedroom No.1 (2) -
ms1mpd1030pm.jpeg, ms1mpd1045pm.jpeg

(By listing your positive evidence by name and time here you have an easy reference to make sure they are in your timeline.)

Audio: (provide this for each recorder used)
Total length of audio recording: 1 hour
Total positive EVPS: 0
Locations of Positive EVPs: i.e. living room (1) - ms1mpd937pm.wav.
Bedroom No.1 (1) - ms1mpd1035pm.wav

(By listing your positive evidence by name and time here you have an easy reference to make sure they are in your timeline.)

Hand Held Video:
Total length of video recording: 1
Total positive video clips: 1
Locations of Positive video clips: i.e. living room (1) -
ms1mpd937pm.avi, Bedroom No.1 (1) - ms1mpd1035pm.avi

Total positive Video EVPS: 0
Total length of audio recording from video: 1 hour *(obviously this needs to match the total length of vide recording with the hand held camera)*
Total positive EVPS: 0
Locations of Positive EVPs:

(By listing your positive evidence by name and time here you have an easy reference to make sure they are in your timeline.) You may also get an EVP from your video cameras list them here.

Digital Video Recording (DVR):
Number of cameras used: 4
Total length of video recording: 12 hours (this is a total of ALL DVR cameras)
Total positive video clips: 0
Locations of Positive video clips:0

(By listing your positive evidence by name and time here you have an easy reference to make sure they are in your timeline.)

Total positive anomalous EMF readings per meter used:
Trifield Natural EMF detector: 0
Cell Sensor EMF detector: 1
KII EMF detector: 0
Osun EMF detector: 0
ELF Zone EMF detector: 0
Digital EMF detector: 0
Mel 8704 EMF detector: 0

Total Positive anomalous temperature changes per device:
Non Contact IR Thermometers: 0
Location of IR Thermometer temperature fluctuation/with range: i.e. living room – 10 degree F rise/drop.
Mel 8704 Thermometer: 0
Mel 8704 Thermometer temperature fluctuation/with range: i.e. living room – 10 degree F rise/drop. Note the time of temperature change as well.

Total Positive Motion Sensor Readings: 0

Before we continuing we need to mention how to word events in a report. Typically your client will not understand what you are doing, what happened or what you are saying in a report, so be consistent and explain some of what happened. Here is an example of what not to say:

9:00 pm – The KII meter changed colors.

What does that mean? Was it Christmas time and it was being seasonal? So you need to explain that in a little more detail and it is really simple. This is how that should read:

9:00 pm – The KII meter located on the dining room table indicated a fluctuation in the nearby electromagnetic field.

That explained what actually happened.

Timeline:

8:30 pm – We arrived at the home and placed our equipment in the dining room area. This will be the base for the night.

8:45 pm – The entire team did a preliminary walk thru to familiarize ourselves with the location and to establish the room identifications. During the walk thru I recorder the following base readings:

<u>Basement:</u> 73 degrees, 0.2 Milligauss (mg)

<u>First floor:</u>
Kitchen – 75 degrees, 0.2 mg
Dining room – 75 degrees, 0.1 mg
Living room – 75 degrees, 0.1 mg
Family room – 75 degrees, 0.2 mg

<u>Second floor:</u>
Bedroom No.1 – 77 degrees, 0.1 mg
Bedroom No. 2 – 77 degrees, 0.1 mg
Bedroom No. 3 – 77 degrees, 0.1 mg
Bedroom No. 4 – 76 degrees, 0.1 mg
Bathroom – 75 degrees, 0.1 mg
Hallway – 77 degrees, 0.1 mg

> (By listing these readings on one persons report you now have the base reading of the entire location for temperature and EMF and this gives you something to measure against.)

9:00 pm – We begin the investigation and I am teamed with Investigator Smith. We are placed onto the first floor to start off. We position ourselves in the living room .

9:03 pm – I placed an ELF zone EMF detector on the center coffee table covering the area in front of the front window. I placed the second ELF zone EMF detector on the opposite end of the coffee table covering the entrance to the dining room. I placed the cell sensor EMF detector on the table adjacent to the entrance hall covering the entrance into the living room. I placed one KII EMF detector on the fire place mantle covering the center of the room. I placed the final KII EMF detector on the sofa next to where I was sitting.

9:05 pm – I use my digital voice recorder in an attempt to record an EVP

9:15 pm – The name of Aunt Emma has just popped into mind. I do not have an Aunt with that name maybe this will have some relevance to the homeowners.

9:20 pm – Investigator Smith is starting an EVP recording so I use my digital voice recorder and record along with him in an attempt to record an EVP while he is asking the questions.

9:27 pm – Investigator Smith has indicated he is feeling a cold spot, I use the non contact IR thermometer to see if there is any significant temperature change. There is not. To double check this I use the Mel 8704 meter with the ambient probe and it indicates no temperature change. I also take several photos none of which had any anomalies in them.

9:30 pm – Investigator Smith has indicated the cold spot has returned I use the non contact IR thermometer to see if there is any significant temperature change. There is not. To double check this I use the Mel 8704 meter with the ambient probe and it indicates no temperature change. I also take several photos again and obtained a positive photo of an apparition to investigator Smiths right - ms1mpd930pm.jpeg

9:32 pm – I use my digital voice recorder in an attempt to record an EVP.

9:37 pm – I use my digital voice recorder in an attempt to record an EVP and recorded the following: ms1mpd937pm.wav in response to the question – "Is this your house?" This is a clear voice of a female answering "yes".

9:38 pm – The cell sensor EMF detector positioned on the table adjacent to the entrance hall covering the entrance into the living room has indicated a fluctuation in the nearby electromagnetic field.

9:51 pm – I use my digital voice recorder in an attempt to record an EVP. I also ask if we can have one of the KII meters indicate a positive reading. We explain if there is a spirit they may be able to wave their hand in front of one of the meters to let us know they are there. There was no response to this request.

9:53 pm – I simulate a knocking noise on the coffee table and while asking for any spirit present to respond by mimicking the sound. There was no response to this.

10:00 pm – We relocate to the second floor.

10:01 pm – I position the cell sensor EMF detector in the hallway. This device has an audible alarm and we will be able to hear it from any room. I also position a motion detector at the top of the stair case to indicate any movement from the stair.

10:02 pm – We positioned ourselves in bedroom No.4

(More time line references to be recorded here.)

10:15 pm – We relocated into bedroom No. 3

(More time line references to be recorded here.)

10:30 pm – We relocated into bedroom No. 2

(More time line references to be recorded here.)

10:45 pm – We relocated into bedroom No.1

(More time line references to be recorded here.)

11:00 pm – We took a break

11:45 pm – We resume the investigation and we are now positioned in the basement.

(More time line references to be recorded here.)

12:00 am – End of investigation

Impressions:
These are something certain investigators refuse to utilize. I have done my version of a scientific investigation for years but I have always noted these impressions. The investigator is the most valuable tool that you have, your instincts play a major role in what you are feeling and how you are reacting to what is happening around you. These are not necessarily "psychic" impression but how did you feel when you walked

into the basement? If your hair rose up on your neck, something was impressed upon you and that is a minimum of what you would list here. The opposite is also true. If you did not have any impressions then state that: *"I had no impressions while on this investigation."*

Conclusion:

This is where the individual that is writing the report needs to explain whether or not they believe the location to be haunted or not. Now to do this properly they must only go by the "physical" evidence that they personally obtained. If they have obtained zero evidence in the form of photos or EVP's or any other relevant evidence such as EMF spikes or temperature changes. Then their response here must say: *"Based upon the lack of evidence I cannot make a conclusive statement to a haunting."*

That would be the end of an individual report. There is a lot of information indicated within it, the better that information is the better you can log and keep track of your research.

The Master Report

In the "official" group reporting method there should be a master report that consists of a full tabulation of the photos taken, recording times etc. This is also where you can indicate any particular items that you have noticed with your experience in the field. An example of that is:

> *We recorded a total of 12 hours or 720 minutes of audio recordings and we did obtained 6 EVP's (Electronic Voice Phenomenon) With our experience in known haunted locations when we have recorded 2 hours of audio and we typically record 1 EVP, here we are right at that average for a known haunted location.*

Below is a template for a formal report that I have used for the past several years

*Formal Investigation Report case No. ********* – Private Home – Philadelphia, PA*

We would like to thank you for allowing us into your home to conduct an investigation into the possible paranormal events that have been reported. Enclosed you will find the individual reports from each of the investigators that conducted this investigation The results are our interpretation of the physical evidence and other impressions obtained during the investigation.

Date of Investigation:
Time: 9:00 pm to 12:00 am
Location of Investigation:

Weather Information: You can get this table below right from the farmer's almanac at **www.almanac.com/weather** you can easily modify the text to match your reports.

Temperature
Minimum Temperature: 60.1 °F
Minimum temperature reported during the day.
Mean Temperature: 74.7 °F
Mean temperature for the day.
Maximum Temperature: 87.1 °F
Maximum temperature reported during the day.

Pressure and Dew Point
Mean Sea Level Pressure: 30.11 IN
Mean sea level pressure for the day.
Mean Dew Point: 60.8 °F
Mean dew point for the day.

Precipitation
Total Precipitation: 0.00 IN
Rain and/or melted snow reported during the day.
Visibility: 10.0 MI
Mean visibility for the day.
Snow Depth

Wind Speed and Gusts
Mean Wind Speed: 7.48 MPH
Mean wind speed for the day.
Maximum Sustained: 9.90 MPH
Maximum sustained wind speed reported.
Maximum Gust
No data.
Maximum wind gust reported for the day.

Investigators on Scene: John Smith, Brenda Gallagher, Brian Jacobson and Chris Fairfax

Equipment Used:
Here you would list each piece of equipment used – This information was on the individual reports for you to refer to.

Physical Evidence:

Photos:
Total number of digital photos: 52
Total number of positive digital photos: 2
Total number of IR digital photos: 25
Total number of positive IR digital photos: 1
Total number of Full spectrum digital photos: 20
Total number of positive Full spectrum digital photos: 1

Audio:
Total length of audio recording: 1 hour
Total positive EVPS: 0

Hand Held Video:
Total length of video recording: 1 hour
Total positive video clips: 0

Total positive Video EVPS: 0
Total length of audio recording from video: 1 hour *(obviously this needs to match the total length of vide recording with the hand held camera)*
Total positive EVPS: 0

Digital Video Recording (DVR):
Number of cameras used: 4
Total length of video recording: 12 hours (this is a total of ALL DVR cameras)
Total positive video clips: 0

Total positive anomalous EMF readings per meter used:
Trifield Natural EMF detector: 0
Cell Sensor EMF detector: 1
KII EMF detector: 0
Osun EMF detector: 0

ELF Zone EMF detector: 0
Digital EMF detector: 0
Mel 8704 EMF detector: 0

Total Positive anomalous temperature changes per device:
Non Contact IR Thermometers: 0
Mel 8704 Thermometer: 0
.
Total Positive Motion Sensor Readings: 0

Team Summary:

Explain ho this evidence relates to the client.

Impressions:
A brief description or highlight of the more impressive impressions felt from the investigators. One point is maybe you as the group's director had known that there was an Aunt Emma that the family recently lost. I would mention here that Investigator Davis had that name come to mind during the investigation. This is where something that may not mean anything to the individual investigator but is valuable to the client.

Physical Evidence summary:
This is where you would mention the statistical information that you have formulated in your investigation.

Conclusion:
This is where a final review of ALL the evidence comes into play. The person in charge of the investigation would need to make a determination based on their experience and the group's evidence as to whether or not the location is haunted. This would be the group's official opinion.

An Important point to make here is that you also need to understand the mind frame of your client. Psychology plays an important part of what we do. If you happen to capture more evidence here than you did anywhere else in your life but you know the client would not be comfortable. You need to find a way to delicately present your evidence. Always make sure you let them know how to get back to you quickly with questions or concerns. You can never forget they are the reason why you are doing this, to help them.

13. Knowing Your Limitations

You would think that this is self explanatory but you would be surprised at how many groups go out and say they can do more that what they can. By doing this they are hurting the client, themselves, and the paranormal community.

Imagine an extreme scenario where someone that you know is in need of a heart transplant. There are steps involved to reach that type of a decision, it is not one that you went to a dentist visit and now you need that heart transplant. The two don't go together, there are steps in the middle that would lead to the final decision and certainly the dentist is not the person to make that decision for you. How would you feel if that were the case?

Now if something occurred while in that dentist office where he notice something not quite right and suggested you see your family doctor which in turn he suggested a specialist to look at you and it was that specialist that said, "We ran every test known to every cardiac specialist in the world and it looks like you need a heart transplant". At this point there is some credibility to you needing that transplant.

The point here is that the dentist didn't make the call on a transplant, he suggested a person with more education and experience in that particular field to help you out. If he attempted to do any kind of heart surgery there would no doubt be a problem, which could seriously hurt you.

I realize that is an extreme example but not one too far off when you think about it. If you are just getting involved with the paranormal you should not delve straight into" heart surgery" or in our terms an extreme case. You really need to turn that over to a group that is equipped to handle that type of case. This means you need to do a little searching in your area for a group that you would feel comfortable with turning such a case over to. Make sure when you reference a surgeon it is someone that you would let operate on you.

When you enter into an investigation hopefully you understand the case before you arrive on the site. If the case is too much for you to handle then you should not be there. This is important to remember and understand, especially as a start-up investigator or group, know your limitations. There is nothing wrong with telling a client you cannot handle their case. In fact most would appreciate the upfront attitude and would graciously accept another group whom can help them without tarnishing your reputation. They would even say that you did help them out. I have always had other groups a phone call or email away that is better equipped to handle certain cases than I am.

There is no shame in passing this on to someone that is more equipped to handle this. If you ask the team you are referring this case to, they would keep you up to date as well on the progress and the client's state of mind.

In a demonic haunting, there is a real possibility of physical harm to someone in your group or to someone in the home you are entering. Go into this case will open you up to the demonic side, a side that will always remember you and will always drop by to let you that they know who you are. This would include entering your home and interacting with your family. I have always said that if someone was going to do the demonic side of this field they really need to understand the hazards they are placing themselves and their families in.

To help you understand what you will be facing you should always send out a questionnaire prior to meeting the client. This will always give you an idea as to what you may encounter. In cases where there may be something you do not want to handle this is the first opportunity you have to see the potential problem.

This is a standard questionnaire that you can find online and there is some valuable information that you can use if you know where to look for it.

1. Address of site:

2. Name of witness:

3. Mailing address if different:

4. Phone number:

5. Email Address:

6. How many occupants at location:

7. How many pets: *If you have any investigators with allergies this is good to know.*

8. Occupants' names and ages:

9. Occupants' occupations: *This will help with possible problems. An example could be a clergy member that may not be aware that stirred something up.*

10. Occupants' religious beliefs: *Potential flag would be if a client recently changed their beliefs.*

11. Time of occupancy at the location: *This can help determine if this was something that they brought with them or was here when they came.*

12. Age of the site: *Yes older homes tend to have any visitors but newer buildings need to be researched to determine what was there originally.*

13. How many previous owners (if known):

14. History of site: (tragedies, deaths, and previous complaints) *Any violent history, suicide, murders, etc.*

15. How many rooms in the site: *This is needed to determine the size of your team.*

16. Has the location been blessed? *When was this blessing? Did the client ask for it to be blessed? Why did they ask for it to be blessed?*

17. Has there been any recent remodeling (if so, what and where): *As little as a color change can affect a spirit that used to live in a home and wanted the home to remain the way they had it.*

18. Any occupants on prescribed medication (anxiety, depression, pain, etc) please list names and medications: *Obviously any drugs dealing with psychosis is of interest. If they are off their medication it could be delusional.*

19. Any occupants using illegal drugs (this will be kept confidential): *Too much could lead to delusions.*

20. Any occupants drink alcohol heavily (this will be kept confidential): *Too much could lead to delusions.*

21. Any occupants interested in the occult: (Ouija, séances, psychics, spells) If so, who and what? *If there is occult behavior occurring there could be some demonic activity.*

22. Any occupants currently seeing a psychiatrist or in therapy (this will be kept confidential): if so, who: *Mental stability is always a concern, if someone is unstable there is a possibility they're seeing things in their minds. This needs to be handled gently.*

23. Any occupants with frequent or unexplained illnesses (if yes, describe): *Some demonic manifestations can affect people with sudden illness.*

24. Have any religious clergy been consulted: If so, please list church: *If clergy has been involved it may have generated more animosity towards the client. E.g. If the home is now occupied by a staunch Christian based family and the "ghost" is Jewish they would not appreciate the Christian prayers.*

25. Has there been any media involvement: If so, who: *If there has been this client may be looking for more than just your help.*

26. Have there been any other witnesses besides the occupants (names and relationships): *The more confirmed credible witnesses the better.*

27. Have there been any odors: (i.e. perfumes, flowers, sulfur, ammonia, excrement, etc) If so, when, where and what: *If you do not want to smell it, it should be a flag.*

28. Have there been any sounds: (i.e. footsteps, knocks, banging, etc) If so, when, where and what: *You are looking for a pattern here, think multiple of three's. Up the stairs 3 times each time, a series of 5 knocks 3 times in a row, etc.*

29. Have there been any voices: (whispering, yelling, crying, speaking) If so, when, where and what: *Are these voices recognizable? Is this person alive?*

30. Has there been any movement of objects, If so, when, where and what: *You are really looking for things that defy the laws of physics.*

31. Have there been any apparitions, If so, when, where and what (describe the apparition): *Be leery of children. Something evil will try everything to get you to feel comfortable, be aware.*

32. Have there been any uncommon cold or hot spots: If so, when, where and what: *There is a belief that spirits draw energy creating hot or cold spots. Knowing the location will help in determining if there is a natural reason for this.*

33. Have there been any problems with electrical appliances: (TV, lights, kitchen appliances, doorbells) If so, when, where and what:

34. Have there been any problems with plumbing: (leaks, flooding, sinks, toilet bowls) If so, when, where and what: *Simple remember clean versus dirty is the same as good versus evil.*

35. Any occupants having nightmares or trouble sleeping: If so, who and when: *This may be indicative of a spirit trying to wear the person down. Try to get as much information as possible on the dreams they are having. What is the frequency of the dreams? (Keep in mind a pattern)*

36. Have there been any physical contact: If so, who, where and what happened: *One person constantly be attacked needs to be studied carefully. The type of contact is very important, a gentle pat or a severe scratch.*

37. Are pets affected: If so, how: *What is the normal behavior for the animal?*

38. Describe the first occurrence of the phenomena: (what and when happened?)

39. Who first witnessed the phenomena? *This can help determine if someone led others to agree with what they "believed" was happening.*

40. What time was the first occurrence of the phenomena? *(Keep in mind a pattern)*

41. What is the witness's reaction during the phenomena? *(Keep in mind a pattern)*

42. Were there any other witnesses during the first event? *(Keep in mind a pattern)*

43. How long is the average duration of the phenomena? *(Keep in mind a pattern)*

44. How often has the phenomena occurred? *(Keep in mind a pattern)*

45. Do any of the occupants feel the phenomena is threatening: If so, who and why? *Relieve as much of their fear as you possibly can.*

46. What do the occupants believe is happening: (i.e. it's supernatural, natural, unsure, etc.) *If only one person believes this, there may be more here than meets the eye.*

47. Do all of the occupants agree on what is happening, do any think its nonsense or not happening? *If only one person believes this, there may be more here than meets the eye.*

48. What would you like to see accomplished from our visit? *This is what you should strive to achieve for your client.*

14. What do We Really Know?

Lately I have been reading a lot of different opinions on paranormal research. Many groups believe orbs are dust. Just as many groups believe orbs are spirits. Same theory applies to EMF meters and even EVP's. Why are there some many different opinions on these items that paranormal investigators base their "scientific research" on?

Simply put, we don't know the answers yet. That is why we do what we do, however we need to do things better. Aside from going out and investigating the places we do, we also need to sit down and experiment with what we do and how we do it. We are not all scientist and I believe many do not even know how to formulate a scientific hypothesis that can be verified. This has to happen in order for anyone in the paranormal community to say they have the answer. Right now none of us do.

The scientific side of what we do really needs some refinement, why, because not many if any at all are doing scientific research properly. The basics of this research are as follows:

- What is the answer you are looking for? – Now be realistic here, don't say I want to find out if there is an afterlife right out of the blocks, I suggest you start with a much smaller goal and eventually lead up to that.

- Research all you can on your topic and develop you own hypothesis as to what you believe the proper answer to be. Don't be fooled, you can change your mind as your research continues.

- Test your hypothesis thoroughly. A true testing procedure will only change one variable at a time; this way, as you are working, you can keep track of what that one variable did to your test. As you go further into this you must remember that you need to run your test over and over to see if you obtain the same outcome. Don't forget your testing must be able to be replicated by others, so keeping clear and concise notes are imperative.

Once you have done this it is time to draw your final conclusion. Make sure you answer these questions while doing so:

1. Do you need to do more research to come to a proper conclusion?

2. Does your testing truly support what you are trying to accomplish (your hypothesis)?

3. Can this be replicated?

4. Be honest on your findings

Remember a quote from Thomas Edison: "I have not failed. I've just found 10,000 ways that won't work". This is telling you to keep trying to get to your answer.

If we follow a procedure similar to this, then we may have a place to start. This is a place where these ideas have factual scientific evidence to support them. Our field needs this to begin in earnest.

Most members of our ever growing community do not understand the basics and immediately begin to have their opinions which they believe are truth. Others read postings on a blog or website and they carry on that mantra. We need to develop our own opinions based on our own research.

The most important thing we all need to understand is this: We don't know anything yet. Everything out there is speculation without sound science to back it up. With that being said both sides of every coin are in play, orbs, EMF and EVP all may have a place in our research or may have no place in it at all. Until we know for sure we cannot discount both sides.

15. The Cost of Ghost Hunting

When individuals get involved with this field they are always excited to get started, to jump right in and start to investigate. Getting started is not much of a factor since you really on need the basics, a pen and paper, a camera (5 mega-pixels or better) a flashlight a cell phone and a friend. Most everyone has all of this right now. So what is the cost of ghost hunting? Here we are talking about the financial implications you can and probably will face at some time.

After a few successful group outings with your friends, you are feeling ready to expand and take on some more challenging cases. You have done all of your studying and have even investigated with an experienced group. So what's next?

Well simply stated you need to get your name out there. Obviously the best approach for that is by word of mouth, and that will come eventually. To get started most groups decide to put up a website. This is where they have their name and let the world know they are here and ready to help. This is a great beginning. You can get some free websites but they do look a little unprofessional. Most reputable groups will have a normal website which they most likely have to pay for. So here is the first hidden cost that you must consider.

Another way of getting your name out there is to make some professional looking flyers on your home computer. Print them out and start placing them at various locations around town. This is pretty inexpensive right? Well let's consider how you design your logo or just a simple flyer. If you have a lot of color or even if you just make the background black, your ink cost will be pretty high. Not to mention the paper that you will be printing this out on. After a couple of printings you will realize, hey this is starting to add up. So if you decide this approach try to be reasonable on your color selections and the black backgrounds. The printing and paper cost can easily surprise you.

Well you made up some flyers and you are starting to create a website. Watch for the pitfalls that many people run into. If you place ghoulish images and scary entities onto your home page you will turn people off that are actually looking for help. People are already scared, that's why they are looking for you. They certainly do not need to see this imagery when they are looking for help to get away from this very thing.

Your website should be simple to navigate through and clearly state what you do. If you are getting involved to help people, let the public know that. Make sure you mention your services are for free. Most investigators are doing this to help people and want to help the paranormal field grow in its knowledge base. One of the most important things to have on your website, flyers or whatever you have your groups name on is how to contact you. An email is great, but what if you have someone in a situation that they want help NOW. A phone number is the best way for that.

A phone number, which creates a new situation doesn't it? I have my cell phone; I will just give out that number. Are you sure that is what you want to do? I would be careful with that approach. The question is, do you want to have your cell phone number all over the place? So here is another potential cost. Some groups set-up a spare cell phone onto their existing cell service and publish that phone number. That is what I did when we first started out. However, there is a cost to do this.

Other groups have created 800 numbers which are tied into the internet and they receive a text message when there is a message. So there is another cost, carry an 800 number and be in control of text messages? These can be as low as $10.00 a month, but this is $120.00 a year that needs to be accounted for. As a co-founder/co-director of a non-profit group, I pay this to keep our number out there.

Another step that many groups take is to have business cards made up. Once again this is something that needs to be looked at closely. Make sure your groups name and contact information is clearly on the card. Now there are many services out there that say "free business" cards. Well as dad always said, "nothing is free."

If you have a logo you designed there are simple charges to "upload" these onto the free card places. Be careful again, watch how these upload and make sure you have them sized correctly. You do not want to receive 500 business cards where everything is blurry!! And don't forget to check the spelling; I found this out the hard way!

You can use the free logos and designs that they offer, but it looks much better when your cards match your website. You really want whatever you put out there to have a similar look. Otherwise you will not look professional. Now the final hidden cost on free business cards is the shipping cost. This isn't that much but it is a cost that needs to be understood.

WOW…We just spent a few bucks just to get our name out there. What else do we need to worry about that can cost us money? The answer is simple; your equipment. If you are going out there as a professional group you will need a little more than a camera and flashlight. This is where you can spend a little as a $100.00 to thousands of dollars. I tell many groups and individuals the same thing, build slowly.

When you start out try to have a couple of EMF detectors and a digital voice recorder. You may need to purchase some software to help you with your photos and EVP's. Most of the time ERVP's are very difficult to hear and need to amplified and have some "work" done to them. There are programs out there to help with that. Some are free and are a good start, most of the better ones cost some money. Some of them can cost hundreds of dollars. Once again find something you can work with and start there.

EMF detectors can cost $15.00 to over $200.00. Start with some of the basics and build from there. Obviously the equipment area is where the funds will start to dip quickly. One final equipment piece that will cost you some money if you decide to utilize it is video. If you have a video camera at home that utilizes night vision via infrared lighting, you have a good start. Otherwise you will need to build this up as well. Don't go out and try to get started with a DVR system, this can cost thousands of dollars. There are plenty of other areas that you will need to spend money on first.

The final cost is one that most people do not consider when getting into this. That is your time. This is not a field where all you do is investigate. You need to take the time to continue to learn, to review your evidence and to provide the proper research for your client. Last but certainly not least, is the time to give to your clients. They needed you and that is why you are there and hopefully why you are doing this.

16. Paranormal Terms

There are literally thousands if not hundreds of thousands of terms that are used in the paranormal. What follows here are simply some of the more popular ones that I have seen over the years.

Paranormal Terms: A

Absolute Energy: An invisible primal life force found in the atmosphere, necessary for the existence of all life in the universe.

Acheri: According to Indian lore, this is the ghost of a small girl. They live on mountain tops and come into villages to spread diseases, mostly to children. It does it by casting its shadow on those it wishes to infect.

Activity: Conscious and unconscious thoughts have an effect on outer manifestations this effect corresponds to the type and kind of thought.

Afreet or Afrit: According to Arabian legend, this is a very dangerous demon. It was once the spirit of a murdered man, who now seeks to avenge his death. The demon's spirit is supposed to rise up from the body of the murdered man.

After-Death Communication (ADC): Any spontaneous and direct communication with a deceased individual, without an intermediary (such as a medium) qualifies as an ADC.

Afterlife: Known as the Other Side, the Great Beyond, Heaven and Hell as well as many other names. Basically, it's the life after this one we're in now. Every culture on the planet has some idea or belief in an afterlife, and what it is like. Some believe that we are reborn, to lead out another form of life on the planet. Others believe that the next life is much the same as it is now, with the same family life and there is enough for all. There is a belief in tribal systems of the Underworld. The place is under the earth and the spirits of the dead live together in villages. Even though there are many, many different ideas, theories, and beliefs about where we go and what we become when we die, there are explanations of an afterlife.

Agent: A means by which something is done or caused, a force or substance that causes a change. An agent in paranormal research is usually a person who unknowingly causes poltergeist activity.

Alchemy: The exploration and application of the sciences, particularly chemistry and the pseudo science of astrology, such as they were understood during the middle ages and early Renaissance period. Alchemists were chiefly dedicated to the worthy pursuit of producing gold from base metals and various materials.

All Hallow's Eve: This was originally a pagan festival of the dead. It was the Celts who started it. Ya see, the Celts had their New Year celebration on November 1st, which was called Samhain. That means "end of summer." This celebrated day was for the Lord of the Dead. Now, it was believed that on the night before November 1st, the mystical veil between the world of the living and the world of the dead was at its thinnest. Communication between the living and dead, therefore, was much easier on this night. During the night, the Celts believed that the dead would rise up from their graves to cause a little trouble in the neighborhood. It was also believed that the Lord of the Dead would gather up the lost souls and re-sentences them to either a year in animal form (this was for the ones that were bad) or another year of death (that was for the good boys and girls). The villagers would make offerings to the Lord of the Dead so he'd be a little nicer to the lost souls. The Celts also dressed up in costumes to confuse the spirits. But, after the Christians rose up and started changes things, different cultures had their own twists and finally it has arrived to what we all know it to be today...Halloween.

Alma: Russian Wildman encountered in Siberia and northern China, generally described as being covered in hair and powerfully built, though shorter in stature and more human appearing than the Yeti. Some researchers have suggested that Alma's may be descended from Neanderthals (Homo Neandertalensis).

All Soul's Day: The anniversary of Siddhartha's death celebrated in respect of all people who have made their transition.

Alpha Rhythm: Electrical activity in the brain (about 10 cycles per second) associated with a state of mental relaxation.

Altered State of Consciousness: This is a term referring to any state of consciousness that is different from "normal" states of waking/sleeping. This include hypnosis, trance, ecstasy, psychedelic and meditative experience.

Amethyst: A jewel that has the vibration frequency to protect the wearer from external negative activity.

Amulet: This refers to just about anything one believes to hold some magic power for protection against things like ghosts, demons, or just about any evil there is. Most are made of jewelry, gold, silver or gems. Necklaces with runes carved into them and religious items are considered amulets.

Ancestral Ghost: A discarnate being that communicates or makes his presence known to an earth bound person who has physic abilities.

Ancestral Worship: Obviously, this is the worship of one's ancestors. They are worshiped as deities. Basically, family will put out food and drink for the dead in the belief that the ancestral spirits will bring good fortune to the family and will protect them from evil.

Angel: A typically benevolent celestial being that acts as an intermediary between heaven and earth, especially in Christianity, Judaism, Islam, and Zoroastrianism. An Angel is a spiritual or celestial being sent to earth to relay a message to a person, serve as a protector or help them in their transition into the afterlife.

Angelic Host: A group of synchronized Etheric world intelligences desiring to offer assistance to civilization.

Animal Psi: Paranormal abilities exhibited by animals, also known as "Anpsi".

Animism: The belief in the existence of individual spirits that inhabit natural objects and phenomena.

Announcing Dream: A dream believed to announce an individual's rebirth.

Anomalous Experience: A term referring to unusual experiences that cannot be explained in terms of current scientific knowledge.

Anomalous Phenomena: Natural phenomena that cannot be explained in terms of current scientific knowledge.

Anomaly/Anomalies: One that is peculiar, irregular, abnormal, or difficult to classify, an irregular image that appears on photos, video, or digital media.

Anthropomorphize: The human centric tendency of imposing human perceptions and priorities upon spirits and other worldly creatures or forces, assuming that all consciousnesses must be akin to ours on some basic levels.

Anti Christ: (Satan). The enemy of man and God who, according to many religious cultures, will establish a reign of evil on Earth which will last fifty years before being overthrown by the second coming of Christ.

Apparition: a.k.a. "ghost," are believed to be the consciousness, personality, soul, or spirit that functions apart from the body and has survived the death of the body. Reports indicate that apparitions indeed act like humans. They have the personality and emotions and act and dress like the person they were when alive.

Apport: This is when a physical object has been transported into a closed space or container, suggesting the passage of "matter through matter'.

Arch-Angels: Etheric world intelligences that have purified their soul-minds from all imperfection before earth came into being.

Artefact: In parapsychology, this is false evidence of paranormal phenomena, due to some extraneous normal Influence.

Asport: This is any object a spirit or medium makes disappear or teleports to another location.

Astral Body: The "body" a person seems to occupy during an out-of-body experience (OBE).

Astral Plane: Believed by some to be a world that exists above the physical world.

Astral Projection: An out-of-body experience.

Astral Travel: Belief or theory that a person's spiritual awareness can temporarily detach itself from the physical body, remaining connected by what is called the "silver cord," and experience things in other locations, time frames or dimensional planes. Some refer to this as "Astral Projection" or "Mind Projection."

Astrology: A science and art that brings guidance and counsel to mankind based on one's birth date.

Atavism: Reversion to an earlier, ancestral type.

Aura: An invisible breath, emanation, or radiation. A distinctive but intangible quality that seems to surround a person or thing; atmosphere.

Authentication: To establish the authenticity of; prove genuine. The verification of facts and details surrounding an occurrence of paranormal phenomenon.

Automatic Writing: This is when you write something without being aware of the contents. Some people use this method to receive messages from Spirits.

Automatism: The theory that the body is a machine whose functions are accompanied but not controlled by consciousness.

Autoscopy: This is when someone sees their 'double', or when they're looking back at their self from a position outside their body (Out-of-body Experience (OBE)).

Avatar: Hindu belief in divine incarnation

Paranormal Terms: B

Ba: Ancient Egyptian concept of a person's essence, believed to be immortal.

Banishing: Formal, ceremonial, procedure affected to cast an invisible presence or influence out from an area. This term can refer either to a spiritual cleansing, or the closing of a magical rite, when the invoked powers are dismissed.

Banshee: A female spirit in Gaelic folklore believed to presage, by wailing, a death in a family. In the Gaelic belief this is a female entity who heralds a death by groaning and screaming.

Baphomet: Demon character supposedly worshiped by the Knights Templar in 14th century France. Some present day practitioners of the black arts regard Baphomet as a "god" of lust and regeneration, or as symbolic of the Devil.

Bardo: In Tibetan Buddhism, an intermediate state of existence, usually referring to the state between life and rebirth.

Being: To exist in actuality; have life or reality, the state or quality of having existence, a living entity.

Beelzebub: One of Satan's chief Lieutenants, considered Satan's left hand man.

Bigfoot: A bulky, hair covered, bipedal humanoid which appears to possess both human and ape-like characteristics. Also known as Sasquatch and Yeti, depending upon locale.

Bilocation: Appearing to be in two different places at the same time.

Bio-PK: Psychokinetic effects on biological processes.

Black Art: To deliberately use psychic energy for evil intent.

Black Magic: The practice of conjuring preternatural forces for a specific evil purpose.

Black Mass: The mass said in honor of Satan at the black witches Sabbath and by Satanist.

Black Shuck: A large spectral death omen demon dog in British folklore, especially in Norfolk and other parts of East Anglia. Black Shuck, also called Old Shuck, derives its name from the Anglo-Saxon term scucca or sceocca, old Anglo-Saxon terms for "demon" or "Satan." The spectral dog descended from Norse mythology, for he is said to be the black hound of Odin (Woden) brought by early Viking invaders.

The Black Shuck is all black and is huge, about the size of a calf. He has large eyes that glow yellow, red, or green as if on fire. Often, he is headless, yet his eyes where eyes should be- glow in the dark. The dog is often thought to be an omen of death.

Bogey(-Man): A grim spectral figure who delights in menacing mortals with rather gruesome pranks and abductions. Although the lore of this character has degenerated into a familiar device used to threaten rambunctious children, the 'Bogey' was formerly soundly dreaded in Celtic regions, and was said to prowl the stretches of fields, marshes, and moors, looking for hikers and travelers who had strayed from their paths.

Brimstone: an element that has all the properties to burn away negative vibrations and evil spirits.

Paranormal Terms: C

Cartomancy: The art of telling fortunes with cards.

Case Study: An in-depth investigation of an individual subject.

Channeling: When a medium apparently allows a spirit to communicate through them.

Cherub: A member of the second order of Etheric world angels, known for their knowledge and help in carrying out the Devine plan.

Chupacabra: Spanish for Goat sucker. In Puerto Rico, for twenty some years, numerous livestock and stray pets have been found with throats torn out, drained of blood and bearing mysterious puncture wounds. On the scene sightings of the creature supposed responsible are exceedingly rare, and descriptions always include "glowing red eyes."

Circle: To make or form a circle around; enclose a group of people who hold séances.

Circumambulism: Ceremonial walking around an object or person to secure protection.

Clairaudience: Perception of messages in thought forms from an entity that exists in another realm. You 'hear' what they are saying in thought form messages. This is a form of channeling. You may actually hear spirits talking or singing in your head yet there is no auditory sounds.

Clairgustance: Awareness of an entity on the other side by the sense of taste. A sense experienced in the mouth. It could by a favorite food associated with a deceased entity, or in many instances the way a deceased person prepared the food to taste.

Clairsentience: Experiencing other realities or entities through one or more of the five senses. Examples: A tickling sensation on the hand or face during meditation or relaxing. A pressure on the top of the head when talking or connecting with a Spirit. Hairs on the back of the neck standing on end when a spirit is near. A sensation in the left side of the face when talking with spirit. A floral smell...like gardenias. Funny how smokers - especially cigar smokers - can be experienced as spirits by the smell of a "good cigar"! A movement as a flick of white, purple, or blue light. Seeing shadows in the periphery of your field of vision.

Clairvoyance: Clairvoyance is the art of 'seeing' with senses beyond the five we normally use. Clairvoyance is often called the 'sixth sense'. It is related to the images that are always present in your mind but you do not connect to. You will experience images, colors, and often animated scenes. In clairvoyance we 'see' with what is commonly called the 'third eye'.

Cleansing (Psychic): A less ritualized form of exorcism, where-in a dwelling or site is purified and malevolent influences are banished through prayers, spoken as the petitioner moves through the area.

Coincidence: A sequence of events that although accidental seems to have been planned or arranged, an occurrence, within a short space of time, of two or more meaningfully related events and without any apparent causal connection between them. Coincidences are sometimes bizarre and extraordinarily improbable.

Cold Spot: An area or place that for an unknown reason seems to be cooler than the surrounding areas. Paranormal investigators usually use thermometers to detect the fluctuations of temperature in a location.

Collective Apparition: This is when more than one person sees a phenomenon at the same time & location. Collective apparitions are good in proving that what was seen was really there, and wasn't just the person's mind playing tricks on them, since more than one person saw it.

Collective Unconscious: Concept put forward by C.G. Jung to refer to a level of unconscious thought and experience shared collectively by humans.

Contact Mind Reading: A technique simulating telepathy, in which the "mind reader" (who generally holds a hand or arm) responds to slight muscle movements produced unconsciously by the person whose mind is apparently being read, also known as muscle reading, Cumberlandism or Hellstromism.

Continuance: Commonly referred to as life-after-death, survival of the psyche post cessation of the biological organism which had generated it.

Control: To verify or regulate (a scientific experiment) by conducting a parallel experiment or by comparing with another standard, to verify (an account, for example) by using a duplicate register for comparison.

Control Group: A group of people whose performance is compared with that of experimental subjects.

Corporeal: Having material or physical form or substance.

Correlation: The simultaneous change in value of two numerically valued random variables, an association between two or more events or variables.

Cosmic Consciousness: A blissful experience in which the person becomes aware of the whole universe as a living being.

Crisis Apparition: An apparition that's usually seen by a person when he/she is at the point of death or is the victim of a serious illness or injury. Also apparitions that are seen in places of traumatic events (Like battlefields) are known to be called Crisis Apparitions.

Cross-Correspondences: Interrelated bits of information received from 'the spirit world' by different mediums at different times and locations. The communications must be joined together to form a complete message from Spirit.

Crossroads: Like when talking about city crossroads, this is where 2 or more things meet/intersect. But when mentioned in paranormal research, we're usually not talking about streets (unless we get lost on the way to an investigation). Crossroads usually mean where two or more lines of earth energy intersect. There is thought to be a good deal of paranormal activity in these locations.

Crossing Over/ Spirit Rescue: Attempting contact with entities, intended to alleviate the entities, distress and aid them in the resolution of their conflicts, and in crossing over to a higher spiritual plane.

Cryptomnesia: Knowledge (acquired in normal ways) that may be revealed without the person remembering its source. Such memories may falsely appear to be paranormal revelations.

Crystal Gazing: Staring into a reflecting surface (e.g., mirror, glass, crystal and liquid) in order to obtain paranormal information; Also known as scrying.

Crypto-zoology: The branch of paranormal research which deals with the exploration of legendary creatures such as Bigfoot, lake and sea monsters, thunderbirds, etc. It should be noted that the Giant Squid (the "Kraken"), orangutans (the "Red Men of the Forest"), Komodo Dragons and gigantic Nepalese elephants all were formerly included in the roster of fabled creatures!

Curse: To invoke preternatural forces to cause harm or injury to a person, place or object.

Paranormal Terms: D

Death: The act of dying; termination of life; The termination or extinction of something. Generally understood to be the extinction of an organism's life, many doctrines assert some form of mental or spiritual survival of physical death.

Deathbed Experience: A dying person's awareness of the presence of dead friends or relatives.

Déjà vu: The feeling of having already experienced something actually being experienced for the first time. An impression of having seen or experienced something before. Also called a Déjà experience.

Delta: A term used to refer to any kind of anomalous experience.

Dematerialize: To deprive of or lose apparent physical substance; make or become immaterial. To suddenly disappear, Example: an object or spirit.

Dematerialization: This word is used to describe a spirit or specter meaning to deprive of or lose apparent physical substance or in simpler terms, without flesh.

Demon: An evil supernatural being; a devil, an evil spirit or being which is said to have not ever lived on earth in human form.

Demonic: Pertaining to or caused by demons

Demonologist: Involved with the study of Demonology.

Demonology: The study of demons.

Deport: The paranormal movement of objects out of a secure enclosed space.

Devil: An upper level evil spirit working for Lucifer.

Diabolical: Pertaining to or caused by a devil.

Direct Writing: occurring most often during a séance, direct writing is a phenomenon in which alleged spirit hand writing appears on a previously unmarked surface.

Direct Voice Phenomenon (DVP): A Spirit voice, spoken directly to sitters at a séance. The sound usually seems to come from a point near the medium, or through a spirit horn or trumpet, but not from the mouth of the medium.

Discarnate: Another word for Spirit, ghost or apparition that literally means "out of body".

Discarnate Entity: A spirit or non-material entity, often used to refer to the personality of a deceased individual.

Disembodied Voice: A voice or sound heard that comes from no physical body or known source.

Dissociation: The act of removing from association; the state of being separate and unconnected. Activity performed outside of normal conscious awareness, or mental processes that suggest the existence of separate centers of consciousness.

Divining Rod: A forked rod (or sometimes a pair of L-shaped rods) used in dowsing.

DMILS: "Direct Mental Interaction with Living Systems". Psychokinetic influences on physiological processes.

Doppelganger: A spiritual or ghostly double or counterpart; an apparitional double of a living person. A mirror image or double of a person.

Dowsing: To use a divining rod to search for underground water or minerals. An act which, generally, a 'dowsing rod' or 'divining rod' is employed to locate subterranean water, ore, oil, etc.. or other concealed items by following the direction in which the rod turns in the users hand.

Dowsing Rods: similar to a Diving rod.

Druid: A Celtic priest of the Bronze or Iron Age, trained in healing, divination and astronomy, whose tradition was passed on to successors by oral tradition.

Paranormal Terms: E

Earthbound: A spirit being trapped on or remaining on the earthly plane

Earthquake Effect: A phenomenon produced by the physical medium D.D. Home, involving the room shaking as if there was an earthquake.

Ecstasy: An altered state of consciousness in which the person experiences great rapture and loss of self-control.

Ecto/Ectoplasm: An immaterial or ethereal substance, especially the transparent corporeal presence of a spirit or ghost. A semi-fluid substance exuded by a physical medium from which materializations may form. Ecto is also what we call the smokey mist like substance we capture on film that we believe to be spirit energy. To avoid false evidence it's important for you and other people to not be smoking during an investigation. If you must smoke, make a place away from the investigation for everyone to smoke at. Also watch out for your breath on cold days, fog, etc.. If you are sure none of the elements above are present and you don't see any mist with the naked eye, yet it shows up on film, you may have something.

Electro Magnetic Field (EMF) Meter/Detector: Also called a gauss or magnetometer, these let you know the Electro Magnetic Field readings in an area. The presence of spirit has been known to often produce/disturb electro magnetic energy in the area. Lots of things throw off EMF's though (Lamps, TV's, etc..) so scout around the area of the investigation first and get to know where these things are. If you start getting fluctuations in EMF readings in an area with no other explanation for them.

Electronic Voice Phenomenon (EVP): This is the capturing of spirit voices on recorders. Try setting up a recorder during investigations (Regular hand held audio tape recorders or digital recorders work fine. If using a audio tape recorder, an external mic is best so you don't pick up the sounds of the gears and such turning of the recorder). When playing the recording back you may hear sounds or voices that weren't heard at the time of the investigation. Try asking questions and pausing also.. you may get answers.

Elementals: In magical tradition and ceremony, spirits which govern the four corners of the earth and are associated with, or reside within, the four basic elements. They are called Sylphs (the east, air), Salamanders (the south, fire), Undines (the west, water), and Gnomes (the north, earth).

Elemental Spirit: A lesser spirit bound to the fundamentals of nature (earth, wind, water, and fire).

EMF, Electro-Magnetic Field: A physical field produced by electrically charged objects, such as wiring, appliances, lights, computers, etc. All objects emit an electromagnetic field.

Empath: An individual who is particularly sensitive to the psychic emanations of his or her surroundings, even to a degree of telepathically receiving and experiencing the emotions of others in their proximity. Obviously, psychic empathy can be regarded as a mixed blessing, and the empath must learn to gain a measure of control over this ability.

Empathic: The action of understanding, being aware of, being sensitive to and vicariously experiencing the feelings thoughts and experiences of another.

Enochian: A magical, "angelic" language first translated by Dr. John Dee, and used in the rituals of both the "Hermetic Order of the Golden Dawn" in the 19th century and the "First Church of Satan" in the 20th century.

Entity: A real being, whether in thought or in fact; being; essence; existence, a disembodied or preternatural spirit.

Ethereal: Heavenly; Not of this world; Spiritual.

ESP: See "Extra Sensory Perception".

Evil Eye: A look or stare believed to cause injury or misfortune to others, alleged ability of some people to harm others by looking at them.

EVP: See "Electronic Voice Phenomena".

Exorcism: A religious or quasi-religious rite to drive out evil spirits.

Experiment: A test carried out under controlled conditions. A test under controlled conditions that is made to demonstrate a known truth, examine the validity of a hypothesis, or determine the efficacy of something previously untried.

Experimental Parapsychology: Parapsychological research involving experimental methods rather than survey techniques or the investigation of spontaneous cases.

Experimenter Effect: Influence that the experimenter's personality or behavior may have on the results of an experiment.

Extra-dimensional: Originating outside our normal space-time reality.

Extraordinary Experience (EE): Describing the occurrence of a wide range of emotionally intense, spontaneous phenomena, such as after-death communication (ADC) or near-death experiences (NDE).

Extra Sensory Perception (ESP): Communication or perception by means other than the physical senses, the ability to gain knowledge through means other than the five physical senses or logical inference.

Paranormal Terms: F

Fairy: A tiny elemental entity [See "Elemental" for more info] considered clever, mischievous, and possessing magical abilities.

Faith: Believing without seeing.

Faith Healing: Healing that is associated with prayer or belief in Divine power.

Fallen Angles: Discarnate entities that live close to earth and are desirous and capable of haunting living people.

False Awakening: When a person believes he or she has woken up, but actually is still dreaming.

Familiar: A live cat or other animal owned by a witch upon which she transfers psychic energy in cases of evil oriented activities.

Fetch: A spectral double of a living person.

Fetish: Aside from the modern sexual connotation, a fetish is a shamanistic tool in the form of a figurine, animal part or a pouch containing items with magical associations.

Fortean Phenomena: Strange phenomena, especially those which challenge conventional scientific knowledge. Named after the American researcher and writer Charles Fort; Fortean phenomena include those generally considered paranormal, but also bizarre non-paranormal events such as monsters and prodigies, extraordinary coincidences, and unusual rains.

Fortune Telling: The practice or art of professing to reveal future events in the life of another, various practices which aim to divine future events.

Fraud: A deception deliberately practiced in order to secure unfair or unlawful gain, the deliberate faking of paranormal phenomenon, generally for the purpose of financial gain, psychological manipulation, or notoriety. Faking for the purpose of entertainment (e.g., by stage magicians and mentalists) is not normally classed as fraud.

Paranormal Terms: G

Gabriel: Archangel who will due God's bidding. A warrior for God that is often called upon to do battle with Satan.

Ganzfeld Experiment: An experiment where input from the outside world is reduced by placing halved ping-pong balls over the eyes and by masking external sounds (covering subject's ears with headphones and playing white noise). A state of mild sensory deprivation.

General Extra Sensory Perception (GESP): ESP in which it is unclear whether the results are due to clairvoyance, telepathy, precognition or retro cognition. Geomagnetic Field: The magnetic field around the earth. Changes in fields are believed to influence spiritual activity.

Ghost: a.k.a. "Apparitions," are believed to be the consciousness, personality, soul, or spirit that functions apart from the body and has survived the death of the body. Reports indicate that apparitions indeed act like humans. They have the personality and emotions and act and dress like the person they were when alive.

Ghost Hunter/Investigator: A person or group who tries to record evidence of spirit or ghosts. This may be done by means of photography, video, EMF (Electro Magnetic Field)/Thermo readings, trying to capture EVP (Electronic Voice Phenomena) on recordings, and other means.

Ghost Hunt: This is the first phase of any case that you will perform, the ghost hunt. Within this step you are going to try to find enough evidence that will support the theory of an active haunting and the need for further research. If the decision has been made to research further; then you have now entered the second phase, the investigation. During this phase you will gather all the information needed to determine the nature and status of the haunting. You will need to know and witness the phenomena yourself, what brought about the activity, the type of entity you are dealing with and what actions and precautions should be taken to approach the situation

Ghost Investigation: A ghost investigation is an attempt to capture spirit activity usually at a location already known, or presumed to be haunted.

__Ghoul:__ Demonic or parasitic entity that feeds upon human remains.

__Globule:__ An anomaly where-in floating, circular forms appear on photographs or videotape, which seem indicative of spirit activity. Globes are a natural containment formation of the meniscus of liquid, as in gas containing bubbles; perhaps the interaction of energy and a quasi-physical substance produced by spiritual manifestations results in a similar effect, the globules being an initial containment of energy. Presently, all we know is that they continue to appear, and extraneous possible causes such as moisture, light refraction or emulsion seepage, etc., have been considered and ruled out.

__Glossolalia:__ Fabricated and non-meaningful speech, especially such speech associated with a trance state or certain schizophrenic syndromes. Also known as "speaking in tongues".

__Gnomes:__ Nature spirits made of pure elemental substance, living underground, in mines and in rocks.

__Goblin:__ A nature spirit showing itself as small, swarthy and malicious, capable of shape shifting to become an animal, thief or villain, name given to the more mischievous and grotesque looking fairies.

__Golden-rod:__ A rare anomaly seen in videotape recorded at the site of a suspected haunting, appearing as bright, white or yellowish lines rapidly moving across a room.

__Guardian Angel:__ An angel believed to have special affection and protection for a particular individual.

__Guide:__ See "Spirit Guide".

Paranormal Terms: H

Halloween: 'The Eve of All Hallows,' also known by Pagan Celts and Wiccans as 'Samhain' (pronounced, 'Sow'-an'), October 31, the night preceding the Catholic Church's 'All Saints Day.' For a millennium, in much of Europe and the British Isles, this was held to be the night when departed relatives were especially remembered, and the veil separating the realms of the living and the dead was rendered thinner than usual. Jack-o' lanterns were placed on stoops and window-sills to frighten off malicious spirits. Halloween is presently celebrated as a night of revels and masquerading, and in Mexico it is part of a traditional annual festival known as 'El Dia De Los Muertos' ('The Day of the Dead').

Haunting: To inhabit, visit, or appear to in the form of a ghost or other supernatural being. This can be sounds of activity, objects being moved, sightings of apparitions, etc. in a location when no one is there physically.

Hellhound / Black Shuck: A spectral death omen in the form of a ghostly dog.

Hex: A magical working, or "spell," cast to influence a person's will or fate, most often referring to a curse rather than a blessing or healing.

Hexagram: 2 interlaced equilateral triangles, one apex pointing up and the other down.

Historic Trigger: It is the human participation in a particular historical/cultural practice that is a tool (not the technological devise) that unearths a "manifestation" that records presence.

Hobgoblin: Mischievous sprite (fairy, spirit) that delights in perpetrating pranks upon hapless humans, once widely believed in and dreaded throughout Europe and Celtic regions. (Caution: It is theorized that these diminutive denizens of the netherworld will, upon occasion, interfere in psychic investigations by devices such as misplacing directions and telephone numbers, draining flashlight and camera batteries, and even pulling keys right out of investigators' pockets!) I assume that anyone who reads the preceding caution will realize it is farcical!

Hot Spot: An area or place where frequent paranormal activity occurs, such as hauntings.

Homunculus: A form of miniature human supposedly produced (for purposes unknown) in the laboratories of medieval alchemists.

Huna: A Hawaiian religious practice involving clairvoyance, precognition, healing, miracles and magic.

Hyperesthesia: An abnormal or pathological increase in sensitivity to sensory stimuli, as of the skin to touch or the ear to sound, exceptionally acute sensory awareness.

Hypnosis: An artificially induced altered state of consciousness, characterized by heightened suggestibility and receptivity to direction. An Altered State of Consciousness involving a heightened degree of suggestibility.

Hypnotism: The act of inducing hypnosis.

Paranormal Terms: I

Illusion: The condition of being deceived by a false perception or belief. An appearance that leads the person to draw mistaken conclusions.

Immortality: Endless life or existence, the belief that some aspect of personal existence survives death.

Imp: A nature spirit that does more harm than good.

Incorruptibility: Not subject to corruption or decay, Inexplicable lack of decay in a corpse.

Incubus: Stemming from medieval lore, a demonic entity capable of sexually arousing and sometimes assaulting human females. Cases of apparent incubus attacks continue to be documented, suggesting a germ of reality behind the myth.

Indirect Voice Phenomena (IVP): Phenomenon in which an entity appears to speak using the vocal apparatus of a living person. Often the voice will sound very different from the person's normal voice.

Infestation: Repeated and persistent paranormal phenomena, generally centered on a particular location or person(s). Also known as a haunting.

Influence: An invisible entity of undetermined nature, affecting the inhabitants of a dwelling. This may initially manifest as an inexplicable feeling of uneasiness, then be followed by more definite signs which reveal a haunting.

Inhuman Spirit: An entity or spirit that has never lived in the earthly realm.

Intuition: A sense of something not evident or deducible; an impression, the act or faculty of knowing or sensing something without the use of normal senses.

Invocation: The act or an instance of invoking, especially an appeal to a higher power for assistance, the act of summoning spiritual beings.

Paranormal Terms: J

Jersey Devil: In the Pine Barrens region of northern New Jersey and New York, for more than two and a half centuries there have been reports of a very strange and singular creature described as having an equine head, glowing, reddish eyes, stork's legs, forelimbs with claw-bearing paws, a pointed tail and membranous, bat-like wings. It emits a shrill, piercing scream, and has been sighted rifling through garbage, standing in paths and roads, and flying just above the tree tops. One rather indistinct photo of this Jersey Devil has produced, but to the best of my knowledge, no one has yet recorded its ear-splitting cry.

Paranormal Terms: K

Ka: Ancient Egyptian term for the astral body.

Karma: A distinctive aura, atmosphere, or feeling, the total effect of a person's actions and conduct during the successive phases of the person's existence, regarded as determining the person's destiny.

Kirlian Photography: A photographic method involving high frequency electric current, discovered by S.D. & V. Kirlian in the Soviet Union. Kirlian photographs often show colored halos or "auras" surrounding objects. The colors in the photographs believe to show several factors such as stress, ill health in living organisms, and the state of your soul. It is analogous to Spiritual Healing which can also be felt but not seen.

Kundalini: In Yogic belief, a source of tremendous vital energy that may be stimulated by various practices. Kundalini, or the "Serpent Power", is believed to provide energy for paranormal phenomena.

Paranormal Terms: L

Legion: The term used to describe a multitude of evil spirits.

Lepke: A very unique and interesting type of spiritual manifestation, a ghost which has the appearance of a solid, living person, may even converse with someone, then suddenly vanish.

Levitation: To rise or cause to rise into the air and float in apparent defiance of gravity. This is a form of telekinetic activity, sometimes associated with poltergeist type hauntings. It is when a person or object is raised off of the ground and sometimes thrown by an unseen force.

Ley Lines: Lines of energy that cross the earth. When two or more of these lines intersect, they form an energy vortex that can act as a energy source of spirit activity.

Lilith: Devil of Sumerian origin and later included in Hebrew beliefs, believed by Quabbalists to have been the first wife of Adam, later excluded from the Talmud, and held by some occultists to be a vampire goddess and a powerful succubus.

Lore: the body of knowledge, especially of a traditional, anecdotal, or popular nature, on a particular subject

Lucid Dreaming: Dreaming in which the person is aware that the experience is a dream.

Lucidity: Lucid dreaming; An early term for clairvoyance.

Lucifer: Name taken from the Latin "luci" (light) and "fere" (to bear), originally a Roman lesser deity, "Son of the Morning," formerly the name for the planet Venus when observed at dawn, in Christian theology identified with the Devil: arch regent of fallen angels. Lucifer is sometimes called upon in pagan ceremonies and rituals.

Luminous Phenomena: The experience of strange lights or glows, often around objects or people.

Lurking Enigma: "Lurk" means to furtively move about, and I can think of no more appropriate term to describe this phenomenon - a type of entity which can be visible to human observers, yet appears in distorted, unidentifiable forms. Common traits reported by witnesses include glowing red or silver eyes, dark color (fur or feathers), startling speed and agility, in some cases winged and capable of flight, as with the 'Jersey Devil.' Although such nebulous creatures seem to mean us no harm, encounters with them can be terrifying, and provoke much curiosity. As one would expect, they are extremely elusive.

Lycanthrope: A person who projects a frenzied display of their innate savagery for periodic episodes, believing themselves to be overcome by the spirit of a beast.

Paranormal Terms: M

Macro-PK: Psychokinetic effects that can be directly observed rather than only inferred from statistical analysis.

Magic: the art of producing a desired effect or result through the use of incantation or various other techniques that presumably assure human control of supernatural agencies or the forces of nature

Magnetometer: A device used to measure the presence of a magnetic field along with its strength, direction and fluctuation.

Mantra: A sacred sound or sacred syllables used in meditation.

Materialization: To cause to become real or actual; To cause to become materialistic. The appearance of spirits in material form.

Matrixing: The natural tendency for the human mind to interpret sensory input, what is perceived visually, audibly or tactilely, as something familiar or more easily understood and accepted, in effect mentally "filling in the blanks."

Medicine Man/Medicine Woman: A witchdoctor or shaman.

Meditation: A devotional exercise of or leading to contemplation. Meditation is the process of relaxing, emptying your mind of all thought or reaching a different state of consciousness. Meditation can aid in spiritual development and/or inner peace. There are many types of meditation.

Medium: A person who professes to be able to communicate with spirits. A person thought to have the power to communicate with spirits of the dead or with agents of another world or dimension.

Mediumship: Activity of a medium.

Mentalism: A branch of conjuring involving the simulation of psi.

Mental Mediumship: The paranormal obtaining of information by a medium.

Mesmerism: The act of inducing hypnosis. The induction of a sleep or trance state, discovered during the work of Friedrich Anton Mesmer, from whose name the word is derived. Also known as hypnotism.

Metal Bending: Psychokinetic ability to bend metal objects.

Metamorphosis: A transformation. See "Shape-shifting".

Metempsychosis: Another term for reincarnation.

Metaphysics: the branch of philosophy that examines the nature of reality, including the relationship between mind and matter, substance and attribute, fact and value

Michael: One of the four Archangels. The St. Michael Prayer, part of the 1884 Leonine prayers (attributed to Pope Leo XIII). It is recited as protection against demons and is part of the Roman Catholic Rite of Exorcism.

Micro-PK: Psychokinetic effects that cannot be directly observed, but only inferred from the statistical analysis of data.

Miracle: an effect or extraordinary event in the physical world that surpasses all known human or natural powers and is ascribed to a supernatural cause

Mist: An anomaly (not usually seen at the time with the naked eye) that appears on photos/videos as a "cloud of smoke" thought to be Spirit energy, also called Ectoplasm.

Mnemonist: A person who has learned techniques that enable extraordinary feats of memory.

Moon Phase: Current status of the moon. Different phases are believed to affect spiritual activity.

Morphic Resonance: A term coined by Rupert Sheldrake to refer to the way in which the "morphogenetic field" (underlying form) of an object or organism may influence
distant fields.

Multiple Personality: A psychiatric condition in which the person manifests two or more distinct and separate personalities at different times.

Mumiai: Native American Indian spirit which behaves in the manner of a Poltergeist.

Mystic: A person who has mystical experiences. Used loosely to refer to psychics, mediums or romantics.

Mystical Experience: Altered State of Consciousness involving experiences of ecstasy, unity, timelessness, loss of self, divine revelation, etc.

Mysticism: Religious or spiritual doctrines which argue that the human mind or soul can directly experience the divine

Paranormal Terms: N

Nazca Lines: In the Nazca Valley of southern Peru are etched enormous tracings of figures of a club wielding man, a splendid spider, a horse, a duck and other figures. Estimated to have been painstakingly etched into the rocky soul more than a millennia ago, these enigmatic representations can be beheld in their entirety only from an Arial viewpoint

Near-Death Experience (NDE): The out-of-body and other experiences people report having when they are close to death. Events within NDE include: an Out-of-body Experience (OBE), life review, a tunnel experience, encounters with spirit guides, seeing dead relatives or friends, a moment of decision (or being told) to turn back.

Necromancy/Necromancer: The practice of supposedly communicating with the spirits of the dead in order to predict the future. A form of prophecy, in which the seer or sorcerer/sorceress raises the spirit of the dead in order to have the wraith foretell future events. It was thought that upon entering eternity, the spirit would have full knowledge of the past, present, and future.

Nexus: the transitional, or joining point connecting physical matter (which, in a sense, is energy condensed) and pure energy, and containing properties of both definite, i.e. the physical brain producing a mind through its network of dendrites and firing axion or the body's connection to the spirit

Noise-Reduction Model: The idea that psi information may be more accessible if normal sensory information (sight, smell, etc..) is reduced to a minimum.

Non-Human Spirit: Spirits that were never actually living. These are often dangerous.

Nosferatu: Slavic, old world term for vampire, meaning "undead."

Paranormal Terms: O

OBE/OOBE: See "Out-of-Body Experience".

Objective Apparitions: Apparitions or phenomena that appear independent of our minds, thoughts, or feelings.

Occult: Of, relating to, or dealing with supernatural influences, agencies, or phenomena.

Occultism: A belief in occult powers and the possibility of bringing them under human control.

Ouija Board: Also known as the talking board. The most popular was invented by Elijah Bond back in 1892. The word "Ouija" comes from the French word oui, and the German word ja...both of which mean yes. This item consists of a flat board with the letters of the alphabet, numbers from 0 to 9, a YES and a NO...all printed on the top. Those who play the game place their fingertips upon a pointer, which then moves "on its own" around the board. Players ask questions and the pointer points to the answers, or spells them out. The game became extremely popular with the rise of Spiritualism, but soon found a more permanent home being associated with the occult. In 1966 the Parker Brothers company began marketing the game as just that...a game for entertainment purposes. Many believe that this board serves as a communication device between the living and the dead. Unfortunately and an often overlooked aspect of this device is that if it truly is a spiritual communication device, the user doesn't know what is truly on the other side, feeding them information.

Oracle: An answer to a question, believed to come from the gods; a shrine at which these answers are given.

Orb: A sphere or spherical object, something of circular form; a circle or an orbit. A sphere of energy looking like "balls of light" on film, thought to be Spirit energy. Balls of energy find in higher concentration in a known haunted location.

Out-of-Body Experience (OBE or OOBE): The experience that the self is in a different location than the physical body.

Paranormal Terms: P

Pact: the belief, prevalent in the late middle ages through the Renaissance, that someone could trade his or her soul in return for worldly gain

Paradolia: a well-documented psychological phenomenon that is both visual and audio. Responsible for the face on Mars and sounds that are even remotely like a human voice will be interpreted as a human voice. If you're ghost-hunting, you'll interpret them as something ghost-related.

Paranormal: Beyond the range of normal experience or scientific explanation. Above or outside the natural order of things as presently understood.

Paranormal Dream: Dreams in which the dream imagery provides paranormal knowledge.

Parapsychology: The branch of science that studies psychic phenomena. The study of the evidence for psychological phenomena, such as telepathy, clairvoyance, and psychokinesis, that are inexplicable by science. (term coined by J.B. Rhine)

Past-Life Memories: Mental images that are believed to be memories of previous lives.

Past-Life Regression: A technique of hypnosis involving regressing people to supposed previous lives.

Pentacle/Pentagram: a five-pointed star, often held to have magical or mystical significance, formed by five straight lines connecting the vertices of a pentagon and enclosing another pentagon in the completed figure.

Percipient: Having the power of perceiving, especially perceiving keenly and readily. A person who sees (i.e., perceives) an apparition or ghost.

Phantasm: A phantom or an apparition. Also called phantasm.

Phantom Lights: can be attributed to blue methane flame produced by swamp gas, or electrical discharges in the form of what is termed ball lightning or perhaps even misplaced fireflies. Yet, in other instances, the phenomenon of floating lights observed over water, the edge of woods, lonely back roads and in the windows of darkened houses just can't be dismissed by ordinary explanations. These might be globules which coalesce and intensify in luminosity to the point where they become visible in dark surroundings

Phasmophobia: The Fear of Ghosts.

Phenomenology: An approach to research that aims to describe and clarify a person's own experience and understanding of an event or phenomenon. A philosophy or method of inquiry based on the premise that reality consists of objects and events as they are perceived or understood in human consciousness and not of anything independent of human consciousness.

Philosopher's Stone: A wondrous beacon of sublime wisdom and awesome revelation, a powerful conjurer's device, perhaps even an extraterrestrial gem encoded with unimagined, otherworldly knowledge. For century's alchemists, mystics, learned men and seekers of truth quested for the fabled Philosopher's Stone, not really knowing where or even precisely what it was. Once obtained, it would impart the wisdom of the world and of the angels. Should this actually exist and is in someone's possession, it may well be regarded as one more enigmatic artifact, since it is unlikely to include instructions!

Placebo: An inactive treatment often given to a control group.

Place Memory: Information about past events that apparently is stored in the physical environment.

Planchette: A triangular device that is used as a pointer on an Ouija board.

Plant Psi: Extra Sensory Perception exhibited by plants.

Poltergeist: This is a German word for "knocking ghost", which means a ghost which seems to move items around a room. The most typical item to look for here is that the same person is around when this phenomenon occurs and decreases or stops when they are not around. Many believe this is caused by emotional and psychological stress in a living individual. Normally this individual tends to be a pre-teen female just entering adulthood. They are unconsciously causing this situation by a subconscious form of psychokinesis. When their apparent issues are resolved the situation seems to return to normal.

Portal: Strong energy gateway between the spirit world and our world.

Possession: Invasion of the human mind by a spiritual or demonic entity, where the invading agent for a span of time, influences or entirely subverts the personality of the human host. It is in these instances that the boundaries of psychology, religion and spiritualism are rendered less distinct.

Prayer: Prayer is an active effort to communicate with a deity or spirit either to offer praise, to make a request, seek guidance, confess sins, or simply to express one's thoughts and emotions.

Precognition: The ability to predict things beyond present knowledge, the knowledge of something in advance of its occurrence, especially by extrasensory perception; clairvoyance.

Prediction: A statement that foretells future events.

Pre-existence: Belief that the personality or soul exists prior to birth.

Premonition: A presentiment of the future; a foreboding. A warning in advance; a forewarning. A forewarning of a future event.

Presence: The state or fact of being present; current existence or occurrence. A supernatural/paranormal influence felt to be nearby. The feeling that an unseen person, spirit or being is nearby.

Preternatural: Associated with inhuman, demonic or diabolical spirits and forces.

Process Research: Research that aims to investigate factors affecting psi.

Proof Research: Research that aims to demonstrate the existence of psi.

Prophecy: A prediction, usually resulting from a sense of spiritual revelation. The ability to receive prophetic revelations.

Psi: Parapsychological phenomena or abilities considered as a group. A letter in the Greek alphabet that denotes psychic phenomena.

Psi-Mediated Instrumental Response (PMIR): Theory put forward by Rex Stanford that psi activity is used to serve an organism's needs.

Psyche: The Greek word for "self", "mind", or "soul".

Psychedelic: Literally "revealing mind". A class of plants and drugs (Example: peyote, psilocybin, LSD) that can produce florid Altered States of Consciousness.

Psychic: A person with above average ESP abilities. Capable of extraordinary mental processes, such as extrasensory perception and mental telepathy.

Psychic Impression: Energy left in an area that can later be "played back" like a recording in time. Psychic Impressions left in an area are not interactive and are often associated with a haunting, called "Residual Hauntings". (Example of a Residual Haunting: When people see ghostly soldiers fighting battles on battlefields, etc..) When a person has preformed events over and over again in a location they tend to leave a psychic impression on the area, which sometimes stays in the location long after that person has passed on. Traumatic events in a location may also leave a strong psychic impression on the area.

Psychical Research: A term coined in the late 19th century to refer to the scientific study of the paranormal. Now largely known as 'parapsychology'.

Psychic Photography: General term used to refer to paranormal photographic images. also called spirit photography.

Psychic Vampire: This is a term for individuals who seem to instinctively draw and absorb the psychic energies from others, usually while conversing with (or at) them.

Psychokinesis (PK): The power of the mind to affect matter without physical contact. The production or control of motion, especially in inanimate and remote objects, purportedly by the exercise of psychic ability.

Psychometry: ESP of events associated with inanimate objects. The ability or art of divining information about people or events associated with an object solely by touching or being near to it.

Pyramid Power: Belief that pyramid shapes can produce paranormal effects.

Paranormal Terms: Q

Quabbala (or Kabbala) : A very ancient and complex system of Jewish mysticism, probably influenced by Assyrian-Babylonian and Macedonian beliefs and existing as the basis of an underground cult during much of the
middle ages.

Qualitative Method: A research method involving the collection of non-quantitative data (Example: observations, interviews, subjective reports, case studies).

Quantitative Method: A research method involving the collection and statistical analysis of numerical data.

Paranormal Terms: R

Radiesthesia: Theories based on the assumption that living organisms emit some kind of radiation or emanation that is capable of being detected using instruments.

Radio Voice Phenomenon (RVP): Receiving the voice of a deceased human over a regular radio.

Raps: The name given to unexplained knocking sounds associated with physical mediumship and poltergeist activity.

Raudive Voices: Intelligible voices recorded on magnetic tape under conditions of silence or white noise which are heard only when the tape is played. A phenomenon discovered by Konstantin Raudive.

Reading: To receive or comprehend. To attribute a certain interpretation or meaning to. To have the ability to examine and grasp the meaning of. Information given to a person by a psychic or medium.

Reality: The term reality, in its widest sense, includes everything that is, whether it is observable, comprehensible, or apparently self-contradictory by science, philosophy, or any other system of analysis. Reality in this sense may include both being and nothingness, whereas existence is often restricted to being (compare with nature).

Rebirth: In Buddhism, the belief that there is some continuity of mind from one life to the next. Buddhism, however, does not accept the existence of the individual soul and therefore does not view rebirth as the soul's literal re-incarnation.

Reciprocal Apparition: A rare type of spirit phenomenon in which both the agent and the percipient see and respond to each other

Recurrent Spontaneous Psychokinesis (RSPK): A technical term for poltergeist activity.

Regression: A statistical technique that enables predictions to be made from a set of data. A technique used in hypnosis, involving suggesting to hypnotized persons that they are returning to an earlier time. Sometimes the regression occurs spontaneously, without suggestion.

Reincarnation: A reappearance or revitalization in another form; a new embodiment. The rebirth of a soul into a new body.

Reike: A type of healing in which the healer is a channel for universal force and energy.

Religion: A religion is a set of beliefs and practices generally held by a community, involving adherence to codified beliefs and rituals and study of ancestral or cultural traditions, writings, history, and mythology, as well as personal faith and mystic experience.

Remote Viewing: An ESP procedure in which a percipient attempts to become aware psychically of the experience of a person, event, of other info located at a distant, unknown target location.

Repressed Psychokinetic Energy: A psychic force produced, usually unconsciously, by an individual undergoing physical or mental trauma. When released, the power causes paranormal occurrences, which often are thought to be poltergeist activity.

Residual haunting: Same time, same place and same thing, each and every time. All buildings, especially older ones are made up of materials that contain iron. What is a tape recording or a video tape made of? That's right, Oxidized iron.

Retro cognition: When a person finds themselves in a 'time warp' of the past, seeing or experiencing events of which they had no prior knowledge.

Revenant: An entity which projects an appearance of being distressed or misplaced.

Ritual: A prescribed event or a particular form or ceremony that is built up by tradition, and with it, a great amount of energy.

Paranormal Terms: S

Sacred (Holiness): Holiness, or sanctity, is the state of being holy or sacred, that is, set apart for the worship or service of God or gods. It is most usually ascribed to people, but can be and often is ascribed to objects, times, or places. The word holy is related to the word whole.

Salt: Symbol of the element of Earth because it's a crystalline substance it can receive on hold Etheric magnetism better than other substances. Many believe it can ward off evil intentions.

Sanguinor: A person exhibiting vampiric tendencies (the desire to ingest blood) and attributes. These may be either contrived or pathological.

Santería: A syncretic spiritualist religion based on elements from the Yoruba religion of Africa, Native American and Roman Catholicism. Found in predominantly Spanish speaking areas, it can be found practiced heavily in the Americas and outlining territories such as Cuba. Priests and priestesses are referred to as *Santeros* and *Santeras* respectively.Similar in aspect to Candomblé, which is found mainly in Brazil.

Satan: Hebraic term for "Adversary," the "Tester" in the Biblical Book of Job, the most familiar name of the Devil, the "Felled Angel" and the "Evil One." Investigators sometimes come across evidence of the activities of satanic cults, who perform animal sacrifices and apparently believe that desecrations and obscenities are devotions to their dark lord.

Scrying: A term used to cover a wide range of divination techniques which parapsychology would tend to classify as types of ESP. Most scrying techniques involve some degree of fixation on a surface with a clear optical depth (crystal ball, a pool of ink or deep water) or on an area which shows random patterns (flames in a fire, smoke), the idea being that subconscious information available to the scrying will be manifested in their interpretation of the imagery or random patterns they see.

Séance: A meeting of people to receive spiritualistic messages. A group of people who gather in an effort to communicate with the dead.

Second Sight: Another name for clairvoyance.

Sender: Another name for agent.

Sensitive: Capable of perceiving with a sense or senses; Susceptible to the attitudes, feelings, or circumstances of others. A person who frequently experiences ESP (Extra Sensory Perception).

Sensory Deprivation: Conditions of greatly restricted sensory input.

Shade: An entity resembling a once-living being (human or animal).

Shadow People: Thought to be spirits or ghosts; usually black in appearance and have no discernible features. People usually see them out of the corner of their eye, and have also been known to be captured on film.

Shaman: A 'wizard' in tribal societies who is an intermediary between the living, the dead, and the gods. A member of certain tribal societies who acts as a medium between the visible world and an invisible spirit world and who practices magic or sorcery for purposes of healing, divination, and control over natural events.

Shape-Shifting: Paranormal ability to assume the form of another person, an animal or other entity.

Siddhis: Name given to paranormal powers associated with the practice of Yoga.

Sidhe: (pronounced Shee) Irish term for Fairy folk, the "little people" who sequester themselves in woodlands and caverns.

Signet: : A seal used officially to give personal authority to a document in lieu of signature, often a ring bearing a personal or family emblem.

Significance: Results of an experiment are said to be statistically significant when they are very unlikely to be due to chance (and hence, in a psi test, are more likely to be due to psi).

Silky: A female ghost which is attired in a rustling silk garment (sometimes seen, other times just heard) and performs domestic chores for a household after the occupants have retired for the night

Simultaneous Dream: A dream whose elements correspond closely with those in the dream of another person.

Sixth Sense: Grasping the inner nature of things intuitively, an ability of perception seemingly independent of the five senses (touch, smell, sight, feeling, taste); keen intuition.

Skeptic: One who instinctively or habitually doubts, questions, or disagrees with assertions or generally accepted conclusions. A person inclined to discount the reality of the paranormal and to be critical of parapsychological research. Generally seeks rational or scientific explanations for the phenomenon. Paranormal Researchers are also skeptics to an extent, but with an open mind. Before we can say it's paranormal in nature, we must first prove that it's not something that can be explained by other means.

Sleep Paralysis: A condition in which a person seems to be awake/conscious but is unable to move.

Solar Flares: Flares from the sun that affect geomagnetic fields

Soul: The spiritual element of a person, generally believed to be immortal.

Specter: An unusual appearing ghostly figure, or apparition, such as a phantom, a haunting or disturbing image or prospect.

Spirit: A Spirit refers to an actual living essence, or soul, of a person that has remained after their physical body has died which usually still retains the entities traits and personality and can communicate with the living.

Spirit Attachment: Some may consider this possession, but in effect, actually is more like an "add-on". A spirit attaches itself to a living person and traveling with them from place to place. It is not technically a possession, since they are usually associated with demonic activity.

Spirit Guide: A spiritual being who is assigned to a particular person to assist them in their spiritual or life journey. It is said that each person can have more than one spirit guide. These guides can be highly evolved spirits of people who have lived before.

Spirit Rescue/Crossing Over: An attempt at making contact with entities, intended to alleviate the entities' distress and aid them in the resolution of their conflicts, and in "crossing over" to a higher, spiritual plane

Spirit Photography: Capturing evidence of spirit on film. Spirit photographs, when developed, show anomalies that were not seen at the time the photos were taken. Examples include orbs, vortexes, ectoplasm mists and, on a more rare scale, apparitions.

Spiritualism (Spiritism): The belief that the dead communicate with the living, as through a medium. A belief system that spirits of the dead can (and do) communicate with living humans in the material world.

Spontaneous Cases: Paranormal phenomena that occur in everyday life, unsought and unexpected.

Spontaneous Human Combustion (SHC): Refers to cases in which a badly burned human body has been discovered in circumstances suggesting that the fire originated spontaneously in or on the body of the victim.

Spook: to haunt; inhabit or appear in or to as a ghost or specter

Spunkies: The sad spirits of unnamed, unchristened or unbaptized children, believed by old Gaelic and English tradition to wander country roads in search of someone

Stigmata: Persons have been observed periodically bleeding from points on their bodies corresponding to the wounds of the Crucifixion. Although the physiological mechanisms which produce this effect are not understood, it is apparently and externalization of religious fervor. Stigmata have been thought to be an indication of sanctity. St. Francis of Assisi was said to have displayed the stigmatic bleeding, and the best documented case is that of Padre Pio (b. 1887, d. 1968).who will name them.

Subjective Paranormal Experience (SPE): Also known as a Subjective Psi Experience. An event in which an "experient" (a person who experiences), receives some sort of communication of information without using one's conventional physical senses and thought to be paranormal in origin.

Subliminal Perception: Perceiving without conscious awareness.

Succubus: A female spirit supposed to descend upon and have sexual intercourse with a man while he sleeps.

Sufism or tasawwuf: A general term for Muslim mysticism.

Supercharged Orb: These are orbs that tend to leave long streaks behind them, probably from them moving so fast. Watch for light sources in the area though.. Moving the camera around quickly will usually produce streaks of light on the photo of whatever light sources are present.

Super-ESP Hypothesis: The suggestion that people are capable of unlimited ESP. The super-ESP hypothesis is often presented as an alternative to the survival hypothesis in explaining mediumistic phenomena (the medium is believed to obtain information using super-ESP powers and not directly from the spirit of a deceased person).

Supernatural: Of or relating to existence outside the natural world. Something that exists or occurs through some means other than any known force in nature. As opposed to paranormal, the term "supernatural" often connotes divine or demonic intervention.

Superstition: The unfounded belief that certain objects, activities or rituals can be helpful or harmful.

Survival: The belief that some aspect of the person (e.g., consciousness, mind, personality, soul)
lives on after death of the body.

Synchronicity: coincidence of events that seem to be meaningfully related, conceived in Jungian theory as an explanatory principle on the same order as causality.

Paranormal Terms: T

Table-Tilting: Mysterious movements of a table, usually occurring in a séance when a group of people place their hands on the surface of the table. Often the movements are interpreted as spirit communications. Also known as table-turning or table-tipping.

Talisman: Objects of various shapes and sizes which are believed to have specific purposes of good luck.

Tarot: A special deck of cards (usually 78) used in fortune telling.

Telekinesis: Paranormal movement of objects. The ability to move something by thinking about it without the application of physical force.

Telepathy: The direct passing of information from one mind to another. The sympathetic affection of one mind by the thoughts, feelings, or emotions of another at a distance, without communication through the ordinary channels of sensation.

Teleportation: A hypothetical method of transportation in which matter or information is dematerialized, usually instantaneously, at one point and recreated at another. A kind of paranormal transportation in which an object is moved from one distinct location to another, often through a solid object such as a wall.

Thanatology: Thanatology is the academic, and often scientific, study of death among human beings. It investigates the circumstances surrounding a person's death, the grief experienced by the deceased's loved ones, and larger social attitudes towards death such as ritual and memorialization.

Therianthropy: The supposed ability to change from human to animal form and back.

Thermometer/Thermo scanner: An instrument that takes instant temperature changes. Used in ghost research to detect cold or warm spots and temperature fluctuations in an area.

Thought Form: An apparition produced by the power of the human mind.

Thoughtography: Paranormal ability to produce images on photographic film (Example: by concentrating on a mental image).

Thought Transference: telepathic transmitting of images and messages from the mind of one person to that of another

Thunderbird: Prevalent among the Amer-Indian peoples, particularly the Algonquin and Cheyenne, are legends telling of immense birds, and raging storms that would come in their wake. Interestingly, reported sightings of birds of truly monstrous proportions persist, most frequently through the vicinity of the Sierra Madre mountain range in Mexico. In the Miocene era, approximately eight to ten million years ago, a species of bird, discovered in only 1979 and dubbed "Argentaevis Magnificens," (which means 'Magnificent Bird of Argentina') soared through South American skies, with a wing-span of 25 feet and weighing perhaps 200 lbs!

Time-displacement: The experience of a time span separate from the native time span of the observer. The phenomenon is sometimes merely viewed and not participated in; sometimes a person seems to actually time-travel to another era.

Trance Medium: A person who enters a state of trance in order to produce mediumistic phenomena.

Transcendental Meditation: A technique of meditation taught by Maharishi Mahesh Yogi, involving the repetition of a sound (mantra).

Transpersonal Psychology: The study of experiences, beliefs and practices that suggest that the sense of self can extend beyond our personal or individual reality. The subject matter of transpersonal psychology overlaps to some extent with parapsychology, but the two disciplines tend to have different approaches and emphases. Parapsychology is primarily concerned to investigate evidence for and against the reality of paranormal phenomena. Transpersonal psychology, on the other hand, is more interested in investigating the transpersonal significance of such phenomena.

Traveling Clairvoyance: An early term for the out of body experience.

Troll: A nature spirit that inhabits the mountains and has charge of their functions, shows itself as a dwarf or a giant, capable of shape shifting, can helpful or capricious and hostile.

Paranormal Terms: U

Urban Legend: A story that has been told again and again of a supposedly true event, but in reality they are based very loosely on actual fact, if any at all. Some of the most famous include alligators in the sewers, a vanishing hitch-hiker, the boyfriend hanging from a tree over the car, Crybaby Bridge and the almighty gravity hill. These are cute for entertainment, but are usually nothing more than that.

Paranormal Terms: V

Vampire: A mythological creature of the night. Vampires are the living dead, a corpse that has risen from the dead. Some cultures believe they are demons, while others think they are ghosts that rise from their graves at night to feed. Through all of the legends, vampires must feed on human blood to survive. They have abnormal strength and are not hurt by normal means. The vampire is killed by wood through the heart or by sunlight. Hollywood has made this creature of myth a pop culture icon.

Veridical: Truthful; veracious. Information or experience that is confirmed by facts and events.

Veridical Dream: A dream that corresponds to real events (past, present or future) that are unknown to the dreamer.

Voodoo: A spiritualist and ancestor religion, originating in Africa, and now found predominantly in Haiti, Jamaica and Cuba. Magical rites, trance states and possession all play a major role in Voodoo.

Vortex (Vortices): A place or situation regarded as drawing into its center all that surrounds it. A photographed anomaly that appears as a funnel or rope-like image (sometimes creating a shadow) that is not seen at the time of the photograph that is thought to represent spirit. Other theories include; a collection of orbs, a 'gateway' to where orbs originate or travel to or a wormhole in time-space. Sometimes camera straps in the way of the lens can produce what looks like a vortex, so to not have false evidence it's best to remove you camera strap.

Vorthr: Norse guardian spirit. This name is the source of the word Wraith.

Paranormal Terms: W

Warlock: Term originally meant "deceiver" or " one who misleads," in more modern parlance has become associated with a male witch.

Warm Spot: An area or place that for an unknown reason seems to be warmer than the surrounding areas. Paranormal investigators usually use thermometers to detect the fluctuations of temperature in a location.

Werewolf: (Old/Middle English word for man = were) A human being capable of transforming into the form of a wolf (or any variety of animals), then back to human; sometimes referred to as a "Shape-Shifter."

White Noise: Acoustical or electrical noise of which the intensity is the same at all frequencies within a given band. A hiss-like sound, formed by compiling all audible frequencies (used in Ganzfield experiments)

Wicca: Witchcraft as a recognized religion, the practitioners of which refer to their system as, "The Old Way" and "The Ancient Religion." Wiccans in their rituals align themselves with elementals and the earth's natural magnetic fields, personified by the names of ancient Greek, Egyptian and Sumerian deities.

Witch: Broadly, a practitioner of the magic arts, spec. a woman who employs charms, herbs and incantations to affect the workings of her will.

Witchcraft: Witchcraft is the use of certain kinds of alleged supernatural or magical powers. A witch is a practitioner of witchcraft. While the term "witchcraft" can have positive or negative connotations depending on cultural context, most contemporary people who self-identify as witches see it as beneficent and morally positive. The term witch is typically feminine, masculine equivalents include wizard, sorcerer, warlock and magician.

Witching Hour: Most believe this is the hour from Midnight to 1 AM on nights of a full moon. It's an important time, for witches reportedly draw their strength from the moon. As for how the "witching hour" affects haunting activity, it is believed that most activity occurs between midnight and 3 AM (known as the Hour of the Wolf). This is when the majority of buildings and private homes are at their calmest. The workers and/or residents are usually asleep or relaxed. Our guard is down and our senses are more aware of our surroundings, since the normal, everyday distractions are not present.

Wizard: A male sorcerer and conjurer who is especially adept and experienced in his craft.

Wraith: An apparition of a living person that appears as a portent just before that person's death.

Paranormal Terms: X

Xenobiology: From the Greek word "Xeno" = strange, the observation/speculation of the biology of very uncommon or unverified creatures. This term has usage in the research categories of crypto zoology and otherworldly aliens.

Xenoglossy: The ability to speak or write in a language that has not been learned.

Xenophobia: A pronounced aversion to people, or beings, of foreign origins.

Paranormal Terms: Y

Yaweh: (pronounced "Yah-vay") According to ancient Hebrew and Quaballistic teaching, the name of God abbreviated to "YHWH," (in Hebrew, pronounced "Yud-hey vav hey"), which is the Tetragammaton, whence is derived "Jehova." It was deemed forbidden to pronounce, or even seek to learn, the full, true name of the Absolute. (The more archeological evidence uncovered which tends to support Biblical accounts, the more arises suggestion and speculation that, approx. 3,000 years ago, a powerful extra-terrestrial presence took a particular interest in a nomadic, mercantile, tribal group of desert dwellers who would come to be known as the Israelites, the "People of God.")

Yeti: A legendary creature of Tibet's Himalayan Mountains region, an anthropoid with both human and ape characteristics, the "Abominable Snow Man." As with its western counterpart, the Sasquatch or Bigfoot, credible witnesses have reported sightings and numerous tracks have been found, but photographs and purported bodily remnants of the creature remain inconclusive.

Yoga: Religious philosophy originating in India. It advocates the use of physical and psycho-spiritual techniques to lead the person to higher consciousness.

Paranormal Terms: Z

Zarcanor: A malevolent spirit which attacks people while they're asleep, inspiring nightmares and sometimes even inflicting minor injuries such as scratches, bruises and what appear to be finger marks. The name is possibly of Slavic origin.

Zephyr: Spirit bourn upon, governing, or manifesting as the western wind.

Zombie: According to Voodoo tradition, it is a person who died and has been raised by a sorcerer. The zombie is a servant to the one who raised him and has no will of its own. Recent research into the phenomena has led investigators to believe this is not really paranormal, but most likely a medical condition. Researchers have found that most zombies are actually poisoned individuals, who are given a "potion" while they are alive. The potion gives the appearance of death, and if made in the right proportions, the person is buried. Later that night, the sorcerer breaks into the grave and retrieves the body. Again, if the potion works the way its supposed to, the "dead" person will come back to life. Sometimes they don't and sometimes they come back with severe brain damage.

Zoomorphism: Representation of a deity or devil with animal attributes.